A Christian in Khaki

Jonathan Greaves

Published by Monk Street Publishing, Monmouth.

Copyright © 2014 Jonathan Greaves.

All rights reserved.

ISBN: 1500687006

ISBN-13: 978-1500687007

Printed by CreateSpace, an Amazon.com company.

Table of Contents

Foreword

Family inheritances may vary greatly: an old clock that belonged to Uncle John, a vase from Aunt May, a special photo taken at a gathering in the past. We often treasure these things not because of the way they look or their monetary value, but because they help to give us our identity. What matters to us most is not the items in themselves, but the stories linked to them that connect us to those who have gone before. 'The clock, handed down by Uncle John was given to him by Aunt Ethel and it was the only item that escaped the great fire.' 'The vase was a wedding gift to Aunt May and Uncle George and they treasured it.' We keep the items, but always on our minds is the real treasure of family stories that link us to people in the past.

The diary of Philip Bryant which Jonathan Greaves received from his grandmother is the war diary of his great-grandfather and in many ways could be seen as little more than a genealogical relic of history; something to be read privately and valued as a link to a family story. Yet, as Jonathan has rightly pointed out, the diary is so much more than that. The stories found in the journal are interesting as family history and, no doubt, provide Jonathan and his family with a better understanding of his great-grandfather's life. However, there is a rich link here to the wider family of faith of which Philip Bryant was a part. More than that, there is insight into an expression of faith and devotion, which may challenge and inspire others.

Of course, at one level, the diary provides interesting reading for those who want to know more about day-to-day life for one soldier in the Great War. As we travel with Philip in the train across France and Italy, we can sense the excitement of local people who greeted the trains with cheers and singing, even late at night. We discover a feel for the camaraderie that existed among the soldiers, as well as the challenges they faced. While many of us have read or heard about the horrors of the battlefields, perhaps we have not given thought to what it would be like to wash in water that would become 'twenty-two deep before the remains were finally thrown away'. Bryant simply commented, 'I was the eleventh, and then the water was – well – pretty solid.'

While the diary is full of such stories of ordinary life, it also offers insight into Christian faith. I dare say that many of us may be challenged by the simplicity and depth of Bryant's prayer life. The references to Christian devotion are not overly sentimental and do not reflect a shallow pietistic idealism which was oblivious to the horrors or sufferings of war. Rather, Bryant reveals a simple, but honest, desire to trust and believe and go forward in spite of the unknown future.

I am grateful to Jonathan for sharing this piece of family inheritance with a wider audience and for giving me the opportunity to commend this work to you. Perhaps in reading it, you, like me, will have the opportunity to reflect more deeply on the faith of those who have gone before us. And to give thanks once again that Philip Bryant's 'Friend' is ours, too.

Karen E. Smith

November 2014

Introduction

A Family Treasure

"Many of the combatants of the First World War recorded the daily events of their experiences in the form of a diary. Some were subsequently published after the war and have become celebrated. Many more, however, remained tucked away in cupboard drawers for years, unpublished and unseen."[1]

In 2005 my Grandmother passed a brown envelope to me containing a handwritten diary. It was a well-worn, hardback black leather "Quaderno" lined journal, containing about two hundred pages. Neat writing filled the book, and inside the cover an outline of chapters had been inscribed. On the following page, a scribbled-out title read "From 'Blighty' to Egypt and maybe back again," and a faint list of names was recorded – possibly friends who had read it, among whom a second volume may have been lost.[2]

The writer was Philip Bryant, my paternal grandmother's father, who had recorded his experiences and thoughts during his short time of service as a conscripted gunner in the Royal Garrison Artillery during the First World War between 1917 and 1918. He was an older conscript, at the age of thirty-four, and newly married. According to his entries, he had written the diary from journal notes, while

---

1 www.firstworldwar.com/diaries/index.htm.
2 Appendix III.

awaiting his return home from Egypt.[3] This was also apparent from the fact that he uses differing tenses, occasional pencil corrections, and altered dates which indicate a post reflection on the diary, as well as a transcription of entries written at the time itself. Although the journal was full, the list of contents indicated two further chapters had been written in a second volume which is now sadly missing.[4]

The journal is of interest on many levels. He eloquently records the long journey from England to Egypt, as well as his part as a gunner in Palestine, serving under the direction of General Allenby with the Egypt Expeditionary Force. His experiences took place during one of the most successful and decisive campaigns of the First World War. Unlike many diaries of his contemporaries, he includes greater detail than mere brief diary entries. He records the sights and sounds of countries, culture and companions he encounters, as well as personal reflection and observations about the war and campaign itself. He records his experience as a gunner, sometimes appointed to fill in as a non-commissioned officer, and then, due to poor health,[5] serving in the wagon supply lines and then acting as a driver for the guns and caring for the animals used in transportation. He was finally sent home and decommissioned in 1919, the details of which are not recorded in the diary, but would have been covered in his lost volume.

Philip is clearly a great observer. He notes small details of interest in clear and descriptive ways, giving vivid cultural and geographical insights as well as observations of army life, troop transportation, and the operation of base camps. In addition, he reveals things about himself. His peace-time employment as a commercial clerk, later to be a shopkeeper and postmaster, also come through in notes about exchange rates and costs of purchases which were of special interest to him. Readers of the diary also discover his appreciation of simple pleasures. He records the small things that he was grateful for, especially when they had been absent. His humour and frustrations come out in his experiences with mules and flies and other

---

3   Part II On the Desert, October 1917.
4   There are two lists of contents. The first list covers the contents of this journal alone up to IV In Samaria. The second list includes chapters five and six which indicates the second volume was written, hence the new contents list, but was subsequently lost at some time, possibly among the readers who read the volume(s). Research into the last reference to Mr Dawbarn of Wisbech did not produce any further light on the subject.
5   He records having severe lumbago in December 1917.

unpleasant and trying situations connected with army life in the Middle East.

However, his tentative title "From 'Blighty' to Egypt and maybe back again," and his stated aims in the diary itself, show that his intention was to do more than tell a story and share his experiences. He was eager to include his own personal thoughts and feelings, along with his inner beliefs and struggles. As such, the diary is less a record of war, and more a record of a journey: both geographical and spiritual. He wanted others to know what it was like to travel with him, and recognise the hardships and boredoms of troop life, along with his own testimony to God's help and guidance in it.

The spiritual dimension to his diary is one of the reasons why I discovered an immediate connection with Philip Bryant, although I had never met him. For me he instantly became more than just a distant relative. I recognised a familiarity in the way he talked about his faith, right from his opening words, using language which came from my own Nonconformist Evangelical tradition. It was especially noticeable in the way he made reference to answered prayer and God's presence and guidance. My great-grandfather was not only an ancestor, but someone with whom, to my great surprise, I shared a spiritual family. Throughout his diary, he speaks in ways that express a personal and experiential faith, including a sense of God's presence and friendship which is typical of the Evangelical tradition of the early Twentieth Century,[6] and one which, in many ways, is still reflected one hundred years later.

In addition to the diary itself, there were two other pieces of paper that had been carefully kept with it which pointed to his life before the First World War, and formed a basis for some additional biographical research.

The first was entitled "My first sermon, preached on Sunday morning, August 26th 1906."[7] This was handwritten on one piece of thin paper and contained the notes of a sermon he had given, based on the text of 2 Corinthians 6v16 "I will walk in them," from which he took the theme of "Walking with God." The second item was a printed letter from the American Baptist Mission Training School in Bapatla in India. It is entitled as a farewell address "To Mr Bryant" from the staff and students of this and other local mission schools who looked forward to his return following training with an American Baptist

---

6   This is outlined in the biographical sketch below.
7   Appendix I.

Missionary Training School.[8] There were a number of personal
signatures at the bottom. Although the letter was undated, both items
originated from a period before the diary was written, indicating an
aspect of his life unknown to his wider family. This prompted the
need for further research into his early life and a discovery of the
spiritual beginnings which are expressed in greater maturity in his
diary during the First World War.

The fact that he desired his diary to be read by others indicates
that he wanted its contents to be known. My Grandmother had read
and treasured this diary and had preserved it with the two additional
items. She enjoyed reading his descriptions of places she herself
visited in her own life, including Southampton and the Solent at the
beginning of his "Journey Out," and of Europe and beyond. She also
found comfort in his expressions of faith in wartime, during her own
battle with terminal illness. She was delighted, when she entrusted it
to me, to know that it would be typed up and made available to
others, especially to members of our family, on whose behalf I have
researched and transcribed it. Though she did not live to see the
finished book, it is dedicated to her memory.

---

8   Appendix II.

Dedication

Dedicated to the memory of my Grandmother, Barbara Mary Greaves, who was Philip Bryant's daughter.

Philip Bryant c.1916

Research and Acknowledgements

In order to publish the diary, and enable a better appreciation of its contents, it was necessary to know something of the author, and the historical context of the diary. Living at least three generations away from the First World War made it difficult to fully grasp the events he described, as well as understand something of the pre-war life the other items pointed to. A wide range of research was needed in order to piece them together, and to provide a broad sweep of biographical details regarding Philip Bryant's life, and of his life as a soldier in WWI.

By presenting some of this information in an initial sketch, it was hoped that it would offer a helpful introduction to the diary and its author. However, it also enables the diary to be printed without any editing, except for the inclusion of footnotes, exactly as he wrote it. The purpose of the footnotes has mainly been to describe terms or situations, both cultural and military, that may not be widely known to general readers, and details of interest which may point to further information. The criterion used has mainly been, that if the researcher needed to look it up, other readers might also have needed to do so. As such, the diary can be read by itself, without the need for reference to the biographical sketch, or concluding chapter, although it is hoped they are a welcome inclusion in the book.

The primary source of research has been the dairy along with the two additional items kept with it. In his diary, Philip Bryant explains his intention in writing it, includes something of his family life, with hints from his earlier life and occupation. The sermon and farewell letter regarding his time in India pointed to a life and career before his WWI military service. Access to enrolment papers and pension records from the National Archives at Kew helped piece together his military history. This was also a useful source for Census records for the decades from 1881 to 1911 which contained details of his family, life and locations.

The artillery unit records called digests, held at the Royal Artillery Reading Room, Woolwich, made it possible to fill in some of the missing part of the diary, and the British Library India Office records were a useful resource for the Public Works Department in Madras and Rangoon, along with other general records. The Imperial War Museum reading room was helpful for examining personal diaries and records. I am grateful to the staff of these institutions for their expertise and assistance.

To place his life and diary in context, many works were helpful and are relied on in the additional chapters of this book. For a thorough history of WWI, John Keegan's *The First World War* was an invaluable and readable summary, although lacking in detail for Egypt and Palestine to which less than a paragraph is devoted. The Palestine campaign is more thoroughly recorded, especially from an artillery perspective, in the *History of the Royal Regiment of Artillery: The Forgotten Fronts and the Home Base, 1914-1918* by General Sir Martin Farndale, KCB.

For research concerning the spirituality of British soldiers, *God and the British Soldier* by Michael Snape is a great resource although it does not place a strong emphasis on the kind of spirituality exhibited in Philip's diary. For Philip's early career in the Royal Garrison Artillery there are published histories of the Regiment including John Headlam's *History of the Royal Artillery from the Indian Mutiny to the Great War 1899-1914 Volume II*. In addition, *Sahib, the British Soldier in India, 1750-1914* by Richard Holmes is one of a number of useful works that piece together life for British soldiers in India under Colonial rule.

The American Baptist Historical Society were able to examine records pertaining to American Baptists in India and Burma, and kindly directed me to useful resources included in the Bibliography. The Borthwick Library in York holds many records of Yorkshire Methodists and was the main source of materials relating to his church life at home in Haxby, and the public archives in York and Northallerton, were also consulted for electoral roll information and other records. A search of records held by Hull archivists revealed nothing in addition to the reference in the Census of 1911 for Philip's time living there, and the Northumbria Records Office also revealed nothing of his time in Seaton Sluice which was anecdotally remembered. The North Devon and Devon Records Offices had information relating to his life post-WWII as a Postmaster in Beaford and in retirement at Sidmouth, and hold records mentioning his life among the Methodists. Philip and his wife, Millie, are still remembered by the older members of the Methodist church in Beaford today. Other less fruitful lines of enquiry were pursued in the search for the missing part of the diary.[9] Philip Bryant's grandchildren, Francis Greaves and Julia Walker, have been able to supply photographs, and memories, mainly of him in older age in Devon. Miss Marian S. Baynes, a university friend of my Grandmother, who remained a family friend ever since, was kind enough to record some geographical and personal details from memory. I am also grateful to Portbury's Funeral Service who kindly looked up the record of Philip Bryant's funeral arrangements.

At the South Wales Baptist College, Dr Karen Smith, Tutor in Church History and Spirituality, offered assistance and encouragement in piecing the book together, suggesting areas of research, and she has been an invaluable source of inspiration in completing and publishing the work. I am delighted and honoured that she was willing to contribute the Foreword for this publication. I am grateful to the church family of Monmouth Baptist Church who gave me the time in a Sabbatical and numerous study weeks to research the book, and especially to Elizabeth Alderson who kindly gave of her time to meticulously check the manuscript in such a thorough way. In closing I want to express the greatest thanks for my wife Samantha and our daughters who exercised much patience and encouragement during the progress of the project, and who share in my Great-Grandfather's legacy of faith.

The following chapter gives a brief sketch of Philip Bryant's life, before, during and after the First World War and is followed by the transcript of his diary. A concluding chapter then pays special attention to his own reflection and spirituality. There are many other aspects of the diary that may be worthy of exploration, such as his interest in the world, and observations of the life and cheerfulness of soldiers in the midst of war. But Philip Bryant states in his opening

---

9   Enquiries to the Wisbech Museum relating to the "Mr Dawbarn" mentioned in the cover of the Diary, and the possible location of part II of the diary resulted in no further information.

words that his main reason for writing his diary was to show how he had "fared," and how his faith in God had helped him. Therefore, a chapter exploring this overall aim seemed appropriate as an attempt to examine what a life of faith meant for him.

Philip Bryant: a Biographical Sketch.

Early Years and Life in India

Philip Bryant was born on 5th December 1881 in an era of rapid industrial discovery and invention. Many technologies taken for granted in the modern world were just being developed, particularly those which made use of electricity and oil. A fresh wave of railway expansion led to considerable improvements in transportation on land, and the design of the steam turbine enabled ships to travel more quickly and efficiently. The internal combustion engine was only just being utilised in machinery, and the rotary washing machine had just been invented. The bicycle was also newly invented, and the Yale cylinder lock had come into popular use. Machine guns, dynamite, torpedoes and barbed wire were all innovations, as also were the first man-made plastics, typewriters, recording devices and moving pictures. Cars, motorbikes, and radar were yet to be discovered. National schooling for every primary-aged child had just become compulsory, enabling every child to have the opportunity for an education, and advances had been made in health with the development of pasteurisation.

In 1881 itself, the Paris Electrical Exposition displayed and demonstrated the wonders of the recently invented dynamo, incandescent light[10] and phonograph.[11] In London the Natural History Museum had opened its doors for the very first time. Alexander

---

10 Electric light. Previously lighting was produced using gas. Philip refers to this invention in a sermon he preaches.
11 The first device able to record and reproduce sound.

Graham Bell produced the first metal detector, film rolls were developed for cameras, and the first automatic player pianos were patented. It was also the year in which advances in the telegraph and communications made the first international telephone call possible.

Writing at a later date, Arthur Conan Doyle set his detective stories in this era, making 1881 the year in which Watson is introduced to Sherlock Holmes. It was the year in which the Revised Version of the New Testament was published, the most important version since the Authorised Version of 1612. Philip Bryant shared his birth year with that of scientist Alexander Fleming, the Russian ballerina Anna Pavlova, William Temple, later to become Archbishop of Canterbury, author P.G. Wodehouse, and the artist Pablo Picasso. Internationally, the Boers and British had signed a peace agreement, ending the first Boer war, and across another ocean, 1881 was the year of the gunfight at the OK Corral and the shooting dead of Billy the Kid.

In this era of rapid technological advance and scientific discovery, Philip Bryant was born in Marylebone, London. His father, John, was a domestic servant from Kent, who moved to London in the 1870s with his wife, Elizabeth, and later became a Railway official.[12] Philip had an older brother, John James, twelve years his senior, who, following work as a coach servant, joined the 41st Company of the Royal Engineers. They also had a sister, Ellen, nine years older than Philip, a brother three years his younger called Jesse, and a sister Rhoda, who was nine years younger than he was.

The family lived at 6 Hatton Street, and then 102 Glengall Road, Kilburn in London. Following his schooling, Philip had become a striker – a blacksmith's assistant, but seems to have aspired to a different kind of life. Perhaps influenced by his brother's military career, on 17th January 1901, at the age of nineteen, Philip travelled to Gloucester where he volunteered for the Royal Garrison Artillery. He became a gunner with the 31st Company of the Western Division, (later to become the 27th Company) service number 6814 and served with 52nd Coy RGA in India until de-commissioned in 1913.

The RGA had been formed in 1899 when the Royal Regiment of Artillery was separated into two regiments: the Royal Field Artillery (RFA) and the Royal Garrison Artillery (RGA). The two regiments were later re-amalgamated in 1921 to be known simply as the Royal

---

12 Millie and Philip's Marriage Certificate 1915, copy obtained from the General Register Office, Southport.

Artillery (RA) again. The purpose of the RGA at the time he joined up was to operate defences with heavy guns at garrisons, forts, and ports and to operate siege offences, whereas the RFA was primarily focused on mobile field units, supporting infantry. The RGA were considered inferior by the RFA for a number of reasons, including the RFA suspicion of the scientific precision needed by Garrison artillery and heavy weapons. Officers who were transferred from Field to Garrison thought of it as demotion, and such a transfer was used as a punishment. In peacetime, the Garrison artillery were more isolated with fewer opportunities for getting honours, as they saw considerably less action, and had less opportunity for training and target practice.[13] However, there was a greater likelihood of Garrison artillery being posted overseas, and there was more pay, and more opportunity to advance themselves.[14] With so much else against joining, these may have been the primary attractions for Philip, and he certainly made the most of the opportunities given.[15]

He spent three years training at Davenport, the new coastal garrison training school in Plymouth[16] and would have learned skills in a wide range of areas including the latest modifications of weapons, ammunition, and detailed mathematics. Calculations were needed to work out how far projectiles would travel, and what angle was needed for the guns to accomplish it. They needed to include the effect of tide and wind for naval targets, and use their skills to identify the kind of ammunition would be most effective against different kinds of ship armour. He would have learned about the production and uses of electricity, since cells were used for firing and for position finders, and night time lighting and telephones required it. Added to these skills were the construction of and storage of ammunition, managing stores, using ropes, moving weapons and even rowing![17]

He then travelled from Sheerness, arriving in Madras, India on 4th February 1904. The RGA served in military defences under British

13 Col. K.W. Maurice-Jones, *The History of Coast Artillery in the British Army* (London: Royal Artillery Institution, 1959), pp152-156.
14 John Headlam, *History of the Royal Artillery from the Indian Mutiny to the Great War 1899-1914 III volumes* (London: Naval and Military Press, 2005), p332.
15 It should also be noted that according to Headlam, there was a shortage of garrison artillery in India, even though, for a time, the armament of Indian coast defences was ahead of those at home, see Headlam, (2005), op. cit. p279.
16 Plymouth was a new school for coastal garrison training Headlam, (2005), op.cit. p309.
17 n.a., *Garrison Artillery Training Volumes I, II and III* (London: War Office, 1905-1910), p11 and also, for the firing of heavy guns, p157ff.

colonial rule throughout India and Burma. The garrison in Madras was based at Fort St George, around which, since 1639, a trading city had been built up for the British East India Company. The garrison is now the location of the Tamil Nadu parliament and still accommodates garrisoned troops. In 1904, the 52nd Company Royal Garrison Artillery[18] had responsibility for operating the coastal defences in the region. At this time, there was one coastal artillery battery in Madras, and two in Rangoon. However, the Madras battery was decommissioned by 1910, so Philip's company needed to go to maintain the existing batteries at Rangoon.[19]

In November 1906, after a time of service there, his company transferred across the Bay of Bengal to Rangoon, in Burma, which had been part of the province of colonial India since 1886. The term "India" was often used to include British-ruled Burma at this time. Although the 52nd primarily served in the coastal defences, they were given other responsibilities. So Philip was assigned to the Public Works Department which managed the advancement of development work and infrastructure throughout India. They administered the labour-intensive projects for irrigation, canal building, railways, roads and other public works and development programs, all of which initially required military support and expertise but eventually came under civil administration.[20]

The *Digest*[21] of his company's service reports that during this time, they lined the streets and fired salutes for various important visitors,[22] participated in the army football league, often coming

18 *Stations of British troops in India*, Army and Navy Gazette, 19th November 1904 states that there were twenty-six garrison companies in India in 1904. Philip must have been posted to a coastal garrison, since he obtained a Naval artillery qualification in this time. See online source: usacac.army.mil/cac2/CGSC/carl/nafziger/904KAC.pdf.

19 Col. K.W. Maurice-Jones, *The History of Coast Artillery in the British Army* (London: Royal Artillery Institution, 1959), p156. Maurice-Jones also notes that coastal defences were expensive to run in peacetime, so the guns were maintained at minimal cost, op.cit. p159.

20 *Public Works Department Madras Presidency 1910-1911 Administration Report*. Madras: Government Press. And Lieutenant General Sir Edwin Collen, Section XI Army, *The Imperial Gazetteer of India, The Indian Empire, Vol IV* (Oxford: Clarenden Press, 1909), p307ff. For other sources see the British Library, India Office records in the Bibliography.

21 *Digest of Service*, 52nd Coy RGA, previously 37th Coy (1906-1910). The Royal Artillery Museum, Royal Arsenal, Woolwich, London, SE18 6ST.

22 Since the RGA was a relatively new part of the army, and members could feel others looked down on them, it was considered very significant when important visitors came, or when special inspections were required. Maurice-Jones, (1959)

second, although they did win the cup competition during Philip's time of service, and won the Burma Athletic Association football league competition 1909. They attended various courses including the annual musketry training, drill, and inspection for their Service Class Firing of coastal defences.[23]

After the completion of five years of service in India, in March 1909, he returned to Madras where he was deemed medically fit to transfer to the army reserve. Soldiers who transferred to the Section B Reserve spent three years living a civilian life, but were required to serve twelve days training per year and needed to be available for mobilisation if required. His record says he remained in India for a year, returning home in April 1910 and was de-commissioned from the army after completing his time on the reserve list in January 1913.

During his time in India, he had at least two formative experiences. The first concerned his faith and the other his health. The former is apparent in his military records, which seem to indicate that he became a committed Christian, and the Farewell letter demonstrates that he also explored the possibility of entering into missionary service. The other key experience concerned his health and personality, since he had what he describes in his diary as a breakdown[24] which left him with "nerves" and an aversion to prolonged loud noises, although he didn't appear to have "gunner's ear," and the noise of the guns and artillery shells did not seem to bother him. These experiences shaped his life and are foundational for understanding his diary, and therefore warrant closer examination.

His spiritual interest was most likely awakened through encounters with the American Baptists who were active in the areas where he was posted: Madras in India and in Burma. Within seven months of arriving in India, a decisive change in his interest in the

---

p159.

23 The company seems to have remained unclassed, except in January 1908 when they qualified for 3rd Class. *Digest of Service, op.cit.*

24 Carey, *New York Times* 31st May 2010 says that "breakdown" was a popular term used from the 1900s to describe a wide range of mental illnesses from mild depression to more serious illnesses. Often it was called "nerves", implying a physical problem rather than mental one which had been caused to the nervous system. As such, the implication was that it would be something to recover from. This is how Philip used the term, and how he understood its ongoing effect. It was often dealt with, without the need for professional diagnosis or help. The modern equivalent would be similar to stress and burnout.

Christian Faith had taken place. On 1st September 1904, his enrolment record was altered, with an official crossing out of his "yes" to the Church of England and the word "Baptist" simply written beside it. For Philip, however, circumstances had resulted in more than a change of denomination. He had publicly and officially identified himself with that part of the Christian family called Baptists, but for him, this would have been a personal awakening of faith. These new found convictions would almost certainly have resulted in him being baptised as a believer in a local church or mission in India. The American Baptist Missionary Union report for 1905 records that thirty-one people were baptised at their English Church in Madras during 1904, and although a roll was not kept of the candidates, it is likely he was among them.[25]

It is just possible that before this time, he may have had contact with Baptists during his youth. The American Baptist revivalist and missionary preacher, George F Pentecost,[26] was ministering in Marylebone[27] during Philip's childhood and youth, and there were a number of active Baptist churches in Marylebone.[28] However, it doesn't appear that these potential opportunities had cultivated any spiritual interest. On the contrary, the fact that he simply marked

---

25 *91st Annual report of the American Baptist Missionary Union 1905* p184. The English Church was overseen by a missionary called Mr Manley in Vepery. The report indicates that there was a revival of spiritual life and Christian activity in the church at that time. Visiting missionaries, including a Rev. James Lyall from Australia and Ceylon had led evangelistic meetings earlier in the year, leading to a number of baptisms, especially from among their Sunday School. The church building was also being enlarged to increase capacity and "much needed ventilation." Their membership was 126, and the report noted excellent prayer meetings, with church members assisting the pastor in the leading of them.
26 G. Holden Pike, *The Life and Work of Charles Haddon Spurgeon, Vol 5* (London: Cassell, 1894), p138, describes Pentecost as a "brother preacher" to Spurgeon at the Metropolitan Tabernacle in 1874.
27 Randall Herbert Balmer, 'George F. Penecost,' *Encylopedia of Evangelicalism* (Louisville: Westminster John Knox Press, 2002), p444 indicates he later became pastor of Marylebone Presbyterian Church until returning to America in 1897. See also Paul R. Dienstberger, *The American republic a Nation of Christians,* (2000) www.prdienstberger.com/nation/Chap8wpr.htm, Chapter 8. Many aspects of Philip Bryant's spirituality are reflected in Pentecost's ministry: for example, Pentecost taught that personal evangelism by the laity and pastoral evangelism should be the more effective methods of evangelism rather than the revival type meetings that were popular at the time. He had also been involved in mission work with the American Foreign Mission in the Philippines and India.
28 W.T. Whitley, *The Baptists of London 1612-1928: Their Fellowship, their expansion, with notes on their 850 churches* (London: The Kingsgate Press, 1928), p288f includes references indicating that there were seven churches, each of which could seat over 600 people and Abbey Road Baptist accommodated 1250.

"yes" beside "Church of England" in his enrolment papers in 1901 was no indication of religious conviction, and certainly showed that he had no Baptist inclinations at the time. Another indication of his lack of spiritual interest is seen in an entry in his diary where he brings an early memory to his mind. It was prompted by the sound of church bells and his recollection of the "blasphemous hours spent in bed on Sunday mornings at home."[29] This statement reveals a clear sense that he obviously felt a distinct indifference to religious convictions in earlier years. It is likely, therefore, that on enrolment he nominally identified himself with the religion of the large majority of soldiers and the British population of the time.[30]

However, service in India led to a definite spiritual change. Whether his official record was changed at his own request, or whether it was required by the army is unknown. A knowledge of denominational allegiance was important for the army in order to allocate chaplaincy, and to allow Nonconformists or Roman Catholics particular permission to be exempt from attendance at Church of England army parades. In his new found faith, Philip may have wished to be excused from Parade in order to worship with Baptists elsewhere. Either way, the official alteration to his records, indicates an inward change in his convictions had taken place, during his early posting in Madras. This faith, born and nurtured among American Baptists in India, was eventually lived out among Methodists in England, when he returned home. Although he thought of himself as a Baptist throughout his life, his diary shows that his real interest was a personal evangelical faith, and he paid little regard to denomination.

In this respect, he was much like other Evangelicals of his era. Across a range of church traditions, they believed they were following the faith of the first New Testament followers of Jesus, free from the

---

29 August 26th 1917 in Italy. Reflecting that he saw the Marylebone church bells as an intrusion into his sleep rather than an invitation to worship which he obviously had taken no interest in. The use of Sundays for going to church for worship and fellowship was an important part of Christian spirituality in the early 20th Century.

30 Michael Snape, *God and the British Soldier: Religion and the British Army in the First and Second World Wars* (London and New York: Routledge, 2005), p140ff describes the requirement for soldiers to attend Anglican parade services, even if there were no real religious convictions of those attending, and how soldiers were generally classed as C of E, unless stating otherwise. The Anglican church claimed a nominal adherence of 70 per cent of British soldiers at the beginning of the First World War. This was slightly more than the 60 percent of the British population who would have been identified as C of E.

layers of ecclesiastical traditions that had accumulated over the years. Evangelicals are often thought to be characterised by five main themes[31] which can be detected in Philip's words and actions as recorded in his diary. In order to understand his comments and outlook, it is helpful to briefly outline them here.

The first of these is with regard to the Bible which Evangelicals like Philip would describe as God's Word. By this they mean that they believe that it is in the Bible that God has revealed Himself and His truth in a way that everyone can read and know for themselves. They therefore study it and try to apply its message to their lives and circumstances. Secondly, they place an emphasis on being Christ-centred. They are not content with a general belief in God, but believe that He entered the world and became human in Jesus Christ. They therefore seek to know God through personal knowledge of Jesus Christ. Thirdly, they place a great deal of importance on the cross. Their focus is not on the cross as an object, but on the fact that they believe the death of Jesus on the cross was the way to mend the broken relationship between people and God. They believe this is what makes the Christian faith Good News for them – the idea that through the cross it is possible to know God's love and forgiveness. However, they also believe that the good news has to be believed or accepted, so the fourth emphasis is that they believe in personal faith and conversion. This means that the forgiveness made possible by Jesus' death on the cross has to be personally applied by turning from what God says is wrong in their lives and putting their faith in Jesus Christ. Finally, they believe that faith in Jesus should make a practical difference, individually and socially. So evangelicals are usually eager to put their faith into practice by both sharing the "good news" with others in mission and evangelism, and by being active in social transformation, in order to see people's lives and circumstances changed.

In Philip's diary, direct and indirect reference to these themes is apparent, especially as a sense of personal friendship with God. It is also clear that he sought to live a life of evangelical devotion and commitment, expressed in a desire to share his faith with others, along with an active concern for social ills and promoting the social good of the wider community. This was the kind of faith expressed by evangelicals whether Baptists, Methodists or other denominations.[32] It was emphasised by the American Baptists in India and their

---

31 David Bebbington, *Evangelicalism in Modern Britain; A History from the 1730s to the 1980s* (London: Unwin Hyman, 1989), pp.4-8.

missionary churches, and Philip would certainly have been nurtured in these themes during his remaining eighteen months in Madras following his Christian commitment.

It was during this time that his first sermon is dated, August 1906, given presumably in a Baptist Mission or church in that region, and again, practical Christian concern of an evangelical nature is expressed there. Preaching continued to be an important part of his Christian service in his early years, and he continued to serve as a "stand-by" preaching steward in later years in the places where he lived in Yorkshire and Devon.

On 13th November 1906, his company was transferred to Rangoon, where he was assigned again to help in the Public Works Department. As well as important from a military point of view, Rangoon was also the headquarters of the American Baptists, and he would easily have had contact with their missions and churches there.[33]

Towards the end of his time in active service, he returned to Madras from Burma, in order to transfer to the army reserve. His record indicates that he expressed an element of annoyance that he was not on the A reserve but the B reserve. The distinction was that A reservists got higher pay, because they were back home and ready to deploy from Britain should the need arise. B reservists were on lower pay because they lived away from home, and were not as readily available. However, the fact he had not returned home also indicates that he had not decided what he wanted to do as a career. The authorities had therefore automatically placed him on the B reserve in April 1909 while he was making up his mind. His medical to transfer to the reserve took place in Madras, with nothing unusual indicated.

The only remaining entry in his military record says he returned home from Rangoon the following year, April 1910, reporting to No. 3 Depot in Plymouth. He says in his diary that his return to Britain was due to a nervous breakdown, though this is not mentioned in his

---

32 In his diary he refers favourably to Salvation Army workers, YMCA work, the work of the evangelical network of Soldiers Homes and evangelical Church of England Chaplains as well as other evangelical people and groups.

33 There was a large American Baptist Church which was influential among British Soldiers in Maulmain, south of Rangoon, along the coast which was also the centre of American Baptist Mission work at that time with a Theological College and a Printing Press. The Printing Press building was newly built and magnificent in comparison to other local buildings nearby at the time, F.D. Phinney, *The American Baptist Mission Press, Rangoon, Burma 1816-1908* (Rangoon: American Baptist Mission Press, 1909), p81ff.

official records. At that time, his company were sent to other areas of the region including Aden and Bombay where coastal defences played strategic importance, particularly against pirates along the coasts of Western India.

Piecing his experiences together for his first year of reserve in India is difficult, but he would certainly have had freedom and opportunity to explore a new career. The farewell letter which he treasured and kept with his diary, indicates that some of his time was spent assisting at the American Baptist Mission Training School in Bapatla, understood by modern readers as a technical college. Bapatla was in the Madras region of South India, and he obviously had explored an awakening interest in missionary work through education.

American Baptist Missionaries had been active in that area since 1840, their first mission station in the Madras region being Nellore.[34] Their missionary strategy was often to establish schools and technical training colleges, the impact of which can be seen in the fact that this area still has some of the highest concentrations of educational facilities in India today.[35]

American Baptist work in the region, including Bapatla, was primarily among the Telugu people who lived there.[36] The school in

---

34 David Downie, *The Lone Star: The history of the Telugu Mission of the American Baptist Missionary Union (Philadelphia: American Baptist Publication Society, 1892)* gives a description of this region and American Mission work there at the end of the Nineteenth Century. See also Helen Barrett Montgomery, *Following the Sunrise: A Century of Baptist Missions 1813-1913* (American Baptist Publication Society, 1913), and Nellie G. Prescott, *The Baptist Family in Foreign Mission Fields. A Mission Study for Adults and young people* (USA: Judson Press, 1926). Helpful maps of the mission work at that time can be found in William Gammell, *A History of American Baptist Missions in Asia, Africa, Europe and North America under the care of the American Baptist Missionary Union* (Boston: Gould Kendall and Lincoln, 1854).

35 At that time, this area had nearly three hundred mission stations, forty American Baptist missionaries, one hundred and sixty local preachers, forty-six churches and nearly three hundred schools. Ongole, nearby, had the largest Baptist church in the world, consisting of twenty-six thousand members: Thomas Armitage, *A History of the Baptists* (New York: Bryan, Taylor and Co., 1890).

36 British Baptists, through the Baptist Missionary Society had focused their work in the North eastern regions of India, based in Calcutta, which was also the headquarters of the British India Office. Their work extended to the surrounding region of Bengal. Canadian Baptists worked further south from here in the Northern region of Madras. The Evangelical Presbyterian Missionary and author Amy Carmichael (1867-1951), (later commissioned by the Church of England Zenana Mission) was also working in this region at the time, especially far south on the southern tip of India, establishing an orphanage there in 1901 which continues to this day.

Bapatla was one of a number of mission schools called "Normal Schools" or "Normal Training Schools" which meant that they were teacher training, and technical colleges. Some were also established as pastor training schools for local people.[37] The Bapatla mission buildings were located on a site near the local bazaar[38] and included the training school, a school used mostly by Hindu and Islamic children and an auditorium for preaching services and prayer. It was also a base from which aid could be distributed and social development exercised. A distinctive feature of the opening of the mission's buildings was that a leading Hindu judge and a local Muslim man were both offered the opportunity to speak and did so, praising the new work, and commending the mission's Christian ethos, expressed in practical compassion and moral guidance which they both believed would be good for the people of India.

In the 1920s Nellie Prescott records some details about the school at Bapatla as she visited it, along with other places, on a journey through India, reporting on Baptist work there. Her record helps see the value and ethos of the schools of which Philip was a part. She describes her journey which had brought her to Calcutta in northern India, and from there she travelled south along the coast of the Bay of Bengal by train to Bapatla.

> *"Here is located the only Normal School in our Baptist Family in South India which trains Telugu men to be teachers. There are about one hundred and fifty students and a large Model School for practise work. These men naturally develop a strong attachment for the school, where they form congenial friendships and where their highest ambitions are fostered and their Christian life strengthened. It is a matter for courage and*

---

37   Rev G.N. Thomssen of the American Baptist Mission was overseeing the work until 1910. He said, when discussing one of the purposes intended for the Bapatla school that 'The great need among the Christian hamlets of South India is for teacher-pastors, and such the school supplies for all the mission.'Helen Barrett Montgomery, *Following the Sunrise: A Century of Baptist Missions 1813-1913* (American Baptist Publication Society, 1913), p136. The work in Bapatla is also referred to in a *Christian Herald* of 1902, which describes the school as part of the work of the "Christian Herald Gospel Hall" in Bapatla because it was built with funds supplied by Christian Herald readers. The Herald article notes that the school and hall were built with the purpose of helping local people improve their lives through opportunity for further training and education. *Christian Herald* (1902) accessible at www.oldandsold.com/articles24/speaking-oak-32.shtml.

38   W.D. Varney, *A Short History of A.B.M Training School Bapatla, prepared for its Fiftieth Anniversary, Feb. 1939* (Philadelphia: American Baptist Publication Society, 1939), p9.

determination to leave all this and go out into a town or village where illiteracy and ignorance are appalling, and to give to the people there a desire for an education and a feeling of need for Jesus Christ."[39]

As Bapatla was expanding, there was a keen interest in obtaining new teachers and this may have attracted Philip as he began exploring a future career. According to the farewell letter, which Philip had kept as a memory of his time there, he had assisted with the general education of the school and had led their Sunday School lessons which the staff and students described as "interesting, full of faith and devotion."[40] His interest in preaching had already begun to be cultivated, but his time at the school also seems to have offered the opportunity to utilise other skills, including his military expertise, since he clearly made an impression as a "tug-o'-war" coach. It was so effective, that within a few days of his being with them, their team had been transformed and were beating better-trained opponents!

It is difficult to pinpoint the exact pattern of his movements over this final year in India. The only clues are the reference in his diary, the undated farewell letter from Bapatla and an entry in his military service record. The timing of the letter is stated to be on the eve of his departure for missionary training in an American school. It also notes that he had been there for only a short time. His diary references indicate that his breakdown took place in India before returning home to England, even though nothing of it is mentioned in his army medical records.[41] Passing references to India in his diary mainly recall the sights of Southern India, including the Nilghiri mountains which is where the British had their hill stations – renowned leisure spots for rest and recuperation, and possibly where he spent time on leave as a soldier, or recovering from his breakdown.[42] He makes no references in his diary to Rangoon or Burma.

39 Nellie G. Prescott, *The Baptist Family in Foreign Mission Fields. A Mission Study for Adults and young people* (USA: Judson Press, 1926), p128.
40 Appendix II.
41 Nervous Breakdown is not referred to in his conscription papers in 1915 as a possible reason for not admitting him into service although this may not be significant, since such things were not closely examined at the time. See reference to Mental health screening for WWI in Thomas W. Salmon, *The Care and Treatment of Mental Diseases and War Neuroses ("Shell Shock") in the British Army* (New York: War Work Committee of the National Committee for Mental Hygiene, 1917) p47. Nor does his breakdown register as placing him among those with "shell shock" as 15% of WWI soldiers had been, see Hans Pols and Stephanie Oak, 'On the Verge of "Vital Exhaustion"? ' *New York Times*, May 31st 2010.

A suggested scenario from this scanty evidence is that having been transferred to the army reserve, he may have then sought work and experience in the Bapatla school while still in Madras. As a result of this, he began to feel a leaning towards similar missionary work, and therefore applied for further training for which he was accepted. Since the letter described his "departure" it implies a journey was needed, in which case he may have needed to travel to Rangoon as his record implies, which was the centre of American Baptist Mission work in the region as there were American training schools locally,[43] or it could well have meant he was destined to train in America itself.[44]

His name is not mentioned in American Baptist records because he did not in the end enter the training the letter described. Whatever the details during that year, something triggered a breakdown, and he returned home to England. Speculation about the cause could cover a number of possibilities, perhaps related to a military situation, seeing something horrific, the effects of loud artillery, or the pressure of study, or it may have been a recognition of the dangerous and difficult circumstances of mission life. It might have been a personal difficulty of some kind. Either way, this period of his life, which he calls his "sojourn in India," filled him with a sense of past regret, and by the time he writes his war journal, his happiest memories are of his new life in Yorkshire, and not his years in India.

Philip also attributes to his time in India the cause of his "thin blood" which, he maintained, made him feel the cold, and be prone to catching them. But in spite of the breakdown, his time in India had been the means by which he found a faith to live by that sustained

---

42 For Hill Stations see Dane Kennedy, *The Magic Mountains: Hill Stations and the British Raj* (London: University of California Press, 1996), especially Chapter 1.

43 In India, at Ongole or Kurnool near Madras. In Burma, the Rangoon Baptist College was in Rangoon city itself – later to become Judson College and the American Baptist Mission Press. Joseph C. Robbins, *Following the Pioneers, A story of American Baptist Mission Work in India and Burma* (Philadelphia: Judson Press, 1922), p36. Also there was a Burmese Theological Seminary at Insein. W. Francis, *Gazetteer of South India, Vol 2* (New Delhi: Mittal Publications, 1988), p425-426 says this was the headquarters of the mission and Robbins, op.cit. p98 that a Theological Seminary was established for Telugu preacher training at the Telugu Baptist Mission in Ramayapatnam.

44 Attending an American Training School could simply mean, rather than travelling to a school in America, that a local American-run college was intended, in contrast to a Canadian or a Lutheran one etc. since many groups had active mission work in the region at that time.

him through the coming war and other personal challenges in the years ahead.

Marriage and the Great War

Having returned home in the spring of 1910, still in the Army reserve, he took up work as a representative for Correspondence Schools. The International Correspondence Schools were founded in 1890 in London, from American beginnings[45] which may have been the connection for his initial interest in them. The role of the representative was to recruit people for the correspondence courses offered, as a salesman, and visit students who had subscribed to courses to encourage them.[46] The courses were aimed at improving a student's abilities, skills and situation, in order for them to be more successful in their own line of work, or even take up a new career.

He lodged in a small terraced house in Hull, with a widow called Margaret Anderson, and her daughter of the same name at 5 Brentwood Villas, Perry Street.[47] He would still have been required to attend a camp of twelve days military training each year, and the Royal Garrison Artillery was active in Hull. Soon afterwards, either his work, or military connections appear to have taken him further north to Seaton Sluice[48] in Northumbria. There was a gun battery at Crag Point which would have been serviced by Garrison Artillery[49] as part of the North East coastal defences. It was here that he met an active Wesleyan Methodist, Millie Smith, from York.

In January 1913 he took up work as a commercial clerk in York after being decommissioned from the army after twelve years of service. It is possible that the correspondence courses may have been the means by which he added to his own education, and his military

---

45 International Correspondence Schools. Now based in Glasgow. www.icslearn.co.uk.

46 n.a., *International Correspondence Schools Instruction papers reprinted* (Montana: Kessinger Publishing Company, 2003), p. 23.

47 1911 Census. Her property is only mentioned in 1909/10 Register of voters. The probable reason for her not appearing in later registers is that the property may not have been valued enough for its residents to be registered to vote.

48 Anecdotal reference from family friend Miss M. Baynes.

49 David J. Anderson, *Hartley to Seaton Sluice 1760 – 1960 The Military Connection* (Seaton Sluice: Seaton Design Group, 1990). Bryant's annual training could have taken place locally, and he and Millie may have met each other if her work brought her to the vicinity, or there may have been a church connection there.

records indicate he had also gained some military proficiency in India. He had certainly advanced his education enough from his humble beginnings in London.

In York, he became involved with Grove Wesleyan Methodist Church where Millie and her family worshipped. She was eight years younger and came from a large family who lived in Park Crescent at the time, later moving to Monkgate. Her father had become a motor engineer[50] and because her mother had died, she would probably have carried the responsibility for the younger children in the family at home. Millie and Philip were married in Grove Wesleyan Chapel on 6th September 1915, by Rev. Henry Bett and lived at 30 York Road, Haxby.

During this time, Philip continued to work as a commercial grocery clerk and threw himself into life with the Wesleyan Methodists. He makes reference in his diary to the deep sense of friendship and fellowship he experienced at Grove and Haxby chapels. The influence of Methodism, or of Millie (or both!), signified a new chapter in his life, for when conscripted for the Great War in the following summer, he described his religion in his enrolment papers as "Wes", and makes no reference to Baptists or their churches at all in his diary.

His WWI diary begins with an entry in August 1916. Philip was conscripted in that summer, not yet a year since he and Millie were married. It was not unexpected since circumstances in the development of WWI had prompted the need for the government to conscript men to fight, instead of relying on volunteers. The complicated origins of the war had drawn many countries into the conflict.[51] By the summer of 1916, the stalemate of trench warfare in Europe had resulted in massive loss of life. Conscription was required

---

50 Census information a decade earlier describes him as an ironmonger's assistant.

51 On 28th June 1914, the Archduke Franz Ferdinand, heir to the throne of Austria-Hungary was assassinated in Sarajevo by a member of a Serbian Nationalist secret society. Following this, a series of international treaties and alliances were triggered, resulting in a world war. Germany, allied with Austria-Hungary and others, later including Turkey, became known as the Central Powers. On the opposite side, a collection of Allies, including Britain, Commowealth countries, Russia, France and Italy found themselves at war with Germany, particularly in defence of neutral Belgium. The USA remained neutral until German submarines became a direct threat to their own shipping and joined the Allies in 1917. See John Keegan, *The First World War* (London: Hutchinson, 1998).

to maintain the numbers needed for fighting there and to maintain other fronts in the East.[52]

Most men between the ages of 18 and 41 were required to serve, and Philip was, of course, also an experienced soldier, only out of military reserve for three years. He was given the service number 382592 and was assigned to the East Riding Royal Garrison Artillery (Territorial Force) Number 4 Depot. They were based in Ripon with headquarters at Easingwold. At this time, it was noted that he had an artillery naval qualification, gained in India, and he therefore became an assistant instructor in gunnery when later posted to Winchester before departing for Egypt.

Mysteriously, he makes two references in his diary to the British campaign in Mesopotamia, as if from first-hand experience, remarking on its haphazard nature and that in spite of this, it would have been more preferable, in his view, to go there than be sent to France. There are also anecdotal family references to his time in "Mespot!". Although there are no official records indicating a time of service in Mesopotamia,[53] the British Campaign was active there from November 1914 and continued through 1917, mainly consisting of Indian troops, initially to protect the oil supply for the Navy fleet. He had completed his time in the army reserve by then, so there is only a very small window of opportunity for service in Mesopotamia following his discharge and before his marriage in 1915. It would not have been post-marriage since his stated occupation on his marriage certificate and on his enrolment papers when "called up" in 1916, was as a grocery clerk. However, since he mentions the disorganisation and blunders of the campaign, apparently from first-hand experience, the most likely possibility would be that he served there before his marriage early in 1915. Either way, a short time in Mesopotamia, if he did serve there, may have given him the opportunity for reflection on life in military service in war time, and was perhaps the reason he kept a diary when called up to serve again a year or so later. Alternatively, his knowledge of the Mesopotamian campaign may have been obtained through a friend, or even his brother if he had served there.

---

52 The conscripts were called Kitchener's Army, since Lord Kitchener devised the idea of conscription and became the face on the iconic poster "Your Country needs you."

53 It is not listed in his Pension, India or First World War records, which means whatever time of service was not considered as eligible for pension income, or the details were just lost.

Philip's service record indicates that on 5th September 1916 he reported for duty at Ripon, the day after which he had a medical examination in Richmond, a further 25 miles away, and was then sent to Great Yarmouth, to the military hospital for vaccinations and some dental work. He then returned to Ripon in Yorkshire, where he prepared for action throughout the summer and on 8th November was transferred to the 1/4 Company East Riding Royal Garrison Artillery base at Haile Sands, on the Humber. Two coastal forts were being built at the time and he noted that the noise of the building works nearly drove him mad!

He was then assigned to the 2nd Heavy Artillery Reserve Brigade at Winchester on 26th June 1917 ready for posting abroad, and commented that he was relieved to have some peace and quiet![54] On enrolment, he had indicated his work was a "Clerk", maybe with the hope, like many, that he'd be given more administrative roles. On 19th July he was promoted to acting bombardier and then reverted back to the rank of gunner on 18th August ready to leave for Egypt and await allocation to appropriate ranks there. This was standard procedure since it saved the need to give higher rank pay during transport to those who weren't exercising those roles. Philip was greatly disappointed to discover on arrival that others had been given the higher ranks, due to the time it had taken for his group to get there.

The Egypt Expeditionary Force (EEF) were fighting "Johnny Turk[55]" and participated in the successful Palestine campaign, in which artillery played a significant and decisive role.[56] His military

---

54 Peace and quiet with Heavy Artillery!

55 British Soldiers called themselves "Tommy" and they called the Ottoman Turkish forces "Johnny."

56 "The Palestine Campaign" covers the operations that took place from northern Egypt into Palestine from early 1917 to armistice in 1918. For four hundred years, the powerful Islamic Ottoman empire had ruled there, and in November 1914 the Sultan had declared a jihad against the Allies. It was a turbulent time in the region. Anglo-Indian forces landed in Mesopotamia (modern Iraq) in order to defend the oil supply for the Navy, but ended up having to surrender and withdraw in Gallipoli in April 1916. While renewed efforts were taking place on this Eastern front, the Allies focused on defending Egypt and the Suez canal: especially following an earlier unsuccessful attack on the Suez by Turkish forces, and a failed Arab revolt against the British in Egypt. See Martin Farndale, *A History of the Royal Artillery: The Forgotten Fronts and the Home Base 1914-1918* (London: Royal Artillery Institution, 1988); F. Duncan, *History of the Royal Regiment of Artillery Compiled from the original records Vol. 1 and II* (London: John Murray, 1879); and W.T. Massey, *How Jerusalem was won, being the record of Allenby's campaign in Palestine* (London: Edinburgh University Press, 1919).

service with 181st Heavy Artillery, described in his diary, covered a geographical area taking in Northern Egypt, Beersheba, Gaza and Jerusalem. The EEF also continued with campaigns into Jordan and Amman to the east, and as far north as Damascus, ending at Aleppo with the Turkish armistice. Philip's recollections of this final period are in the lost part of the diary, and his military records indicate that he remained in Palestine and Samaria until the end of the war. On 9th October, 1918 his company were assigned to the coastal defences at Haifa until returning home in 1919.[57]

Unlike many conscripts, he was relieved not to be posted to France, even though its main appeal was being closer to home,[58] because he felt the cold, and dreaded the trauma of front line noise. He anticipated that it would be quieter and warmer in Egypt, even though it was much further from home and he would be away for much longer. His hopes were confirmed. The Palestine campaign did not rely on trench warfare as in Europe, and there was therefore much less relentless noise of front line weapons.

Apart from those aspects of the EEF campaigns which were made famous by the efforts of T.E. Lawrence in Arabia, the Palestine campaign was lesser known, though of some significance in the war because of the victories accomplished under the oversight of General Allenby. It especially included the capture of Jerusalem. However, while serving an important role in the war, some political consequences of these campaigns led to the formation of many of the modern Middle Eastern nations and in a few more decades, the State of Israel, with subsequent complications in the region today. Many at the time thought of the EEF as a sideline, and some suspected the servicemen of having a "cushy" time in the sunshine. Woodward notes that some thought of those in Egypt as "one degree better than a conscientious objector," adding that nothing could be further from the truth.[59]

Following his Winchester training, Philip describes in detail the journey from Southampton by boat, through France and Italy by train, and the weeks spent awaiting transport to Egypt from the army

---

57 *95th Heavy Artillery Group (H.A.G.) Digest* 1919, The Royal Artillery Museum, Royal Arsenal, Woolwich, London, SE18 6ST.
58 David Woodward, *Hell in the Holy Land: World War I in the Middle East* (Kentucky: American University Press, 2006), p185-186 cites, for example, *Buxton* letter to his mother in August 1918.
59 David Woodward, *Forgotten Soldiers of the First World War* (Stroud: Tempus, 2007), p11.

base in Cimino in South West Italy. His route then took him by ship, across the Mediterranean, arriving in Egypt on 21st October 1917. He was posted to the 181st Heavy Battery Royal Garrison Artillery, Territorial Force. He described them as a "cockney battery", who had just arrived from Salonika where they had been fighting with little success between January and August 1917.

Although Philip was enlisted as a gunner and driver (of horses), he initially worked with the gun detachment, and didn't actually do any "driving" until assigned to the wagon lines, where he worked with the mules and horses pulling the heavy guns and ammunition trailers. The 181st Heavy Artillery Battery used "sixty pounder" weapons, and were part of the 96th Heavy Artillery Group for the Order of Battle in Palestine in the XX Corps, all of whom served under direction of Brigadier-General A.H. Short in Autumn 1917.[60] Before the First World War, artillery had usually been deployed on the front line in the field, or in garrisons. But Generals increasingly discovered the effectiveness of using garrison artillery in support of troops from behind the lines, to destroy enemy targets, rather than on the front line itself. This innovation required a number of new skills since the long distances meant that targets had to be spotted and careful mathematical calculation was needed to fire shells so that they would reach their intended destination. Fire discipline and tactics were an essential part of the Regiment of Royal Garrison Artillery,[61] although adaptability to different conditions on operations was needed. Innovation and adaptation were both things Philip approved of.[62] There were a number of risks for RGA gunners. Although they usually fired from a distance away from the front line, they still remained vulnerable to enemy artillery. The "spotters" who had to go forward to observation posts in order to identify targets were also potential targets from enemy fire, and at the gun itself, mistakes in the firing process could

60 Martin Farndale, *A History of the Royal Artillery: The Forgotten Fronts and the Home Base 1914-1918* (London: Royal Artillery Institution, 1988), p96.
61 For example, n.a., *Regulations for the equipment of the Regular Army. Part 2 – Section XII, Garrison Artillery, Special Instructions and Details.* (London: War Office,1899).
62 E.g. Diary Entry: Shellal. Headlam records that from 1900, the threat of German port attacks meant that considerable upgrades of coastal defences were taking place, with the introduction of large-scale sights for distance and accuracy. "There was scarcely a year from 1904 to 1914 which did not bring some modification of the gear – if it were only with the object of minimising the intolerable din made by the shield doors and trolley wheels," John Headlam, *History of the Royal Artillery from the Indian Mutiny to the Great War 1899-1914 Volume II* (London: Naval and Military Press, 2005), p274. Headlam also notes that there was innovation in the use of high explosive bursting charges for guns, op.cit. p279.

mean a gun misfiring. Gunners could be injured or killed through even a small oversight of one team member, so there was a great sense of teamwork and trust which were essential for effective artillery units, as well as skill and precision.[63]

Philip was in a detachment successfully taking Beersheba from Turkish control in a surprise attack in later October,[64] even though, as he describes, the lack of drinking water made this part of the campaign difficult. Farndale notes that the majority of gunners in the XX and XXI Corps of this campaign were territorial troops like Philip's, but they were well co-ordinated and made a considerable contribution to its successes. He also records how the Allies' accomplishments were partly due to the remarkable ability of troops, including artillery, to move with great speed, and survive on few provisions. This was a considerable achievement considering the terrain.[65] It is acknowledged that the skilful tactics of General Allenby were a leading factor in the success of the Palestine Campaign. Among other aspects, he used artillery as a vital part of his overall strategy. Farndale pays tribute to the effectiveness of his massive logistical organisation which resupplied advancing troops with ammunition and vital provisions. The British artillery were also well trained having superior skills than their opponents, and combined with careful deployment, they were generally more effective than the Turkish artillery forces.[66]

Philip also describes his unit's role in the battles around Gaza. Once captured, the Ottoman Army retreated northwards. Philip's Corps remained in defensive roles around Gaza while the XXI Corps pressed on to Jerusalem. Within one week the EEF advanced fifty miles northwards, capturing Jaffa on 14th November and resisting counter-attacks by the Turks along the way. During the following

---

63 Dale Clarke, *British Artillery 1914-19, Heavy Artillery* (Oxford: Osprey Publishing, 2005). Also see I.V. Hogg, and L.F. Thurston, *British Artillery Weapons and Ammunition 1914-1918* (London: Ian Allen, 1972), p209 for a description of ammunition and firing process for the 60 pounder weapon. www.hackneygunners.co.uk/the-gun-battery/the-gun/ has an excellent section on the 60 pounder gun and its use. The Imperial War Museum, *Image Q 24285* is an online image of WWI gunners in Mesopotamia covering their ears when firing a 60 pounder gun: www.iwm.org.uk/collections/item/object/205091079.
64 Martin Farndale, *A History of the Royal Artillery: The Forgotten Fronts and the Home Base 1914-1918* (London: Royal Artillery Institution, 1988), p98.
65 Farndale (1988) op.cit. p109. Cavalry and artillery were vital in this region since battles were waged on plains and against fortified towns and cities, rather than the stalemate of trench warfare in the European campaigns.
66 Farndale (1988) ibid.

weeks, battles took place across Jaffa and the Judean Hills surrounding Jerusalem, and the Ottoman forces finally retreated from Jerusalem which the British occupied on 9th December 1917.[67]During the winter, due to severe lumbago, Philip was assigned as an animal driver to the wagon lines, and then as a driver of the guns. His diary describes his experiences in his closer role with animals. By this time, being the rainy season, it had become quite cold and wet, and the sheer misery of life in these conditions comes across from his entries.

The role of animals in the First World War has now been well documented.[68] The lack of the kind of machinery now known in modern warfare, meant that animals were essential for transporting food, supplies and heavy weapons as well as for cavalry units who still played a crucial role in WWI battles.[69] In the First World War as a whole, it is estimated that about eight million horses and mules died from enemy attack, illness and exhaustion. Philip became familiar with horses, mules and camels, all of which were needed in the battle field.[70]Artillery guns were heavy and typically required at least four horses to pull the carts on which they were mounted. Horses were also essential to pull ammunition carts and other supplies. Even so, in the mud and cold the animals suffered when wheels got stuck and they still faced the same dangers as soldiers in warfare, getting killed or injured along with troops. Philip's first experience of the actual

---

67   General Allenby famously insisted on dismounting from his horse, and walking into Jerusalem on foot, through the Jaffa (known locally as the "friend") gate, out of respect for the Holy City, and to encourage the concept of coming as a friend to all three major religions to whom the city is holy, rather than entering as a conqueror.

68   See for example, Juliet Gardiner, *The Animals' War: Animals in Wartime from the First World War to the Present Day* (London: Portrait, 2006).

69   Cavalry were especially important in the Palestinian campaign, since so much of the area was sand, and a camel corps had been formed to serve alongside the normal horse mounted Cavalry. R.M. Downes, *The Australian Army Medical Services in the war of 1914-1918 - Part II in Volume I (2nd Ed.)* (Canberra: Australian War Memorial, 1938), Preface and Letters where he felt the frustration of being Cavalry on the sidelines in the Western front.

70   The animals themselves needed proper care, just as troops did. Water was provided along with food and medical care for animals, and their wellbeing was an important factor for the success and strategy of military campaigns. The veterinary corps had a vital role. The war correspondent Massey, noted that for the XX Corps in the EEF (of which Philip Bryant was a part), "the supply of water alone [to the troops, required] 6000 camels and 73 lorries. To feed these water camels alone needed a big convoy." W.T. Massey, *How Jerusalem was won, being the record of Allenby's campaign in Palestine* (London: Edinburgh University Press, 1919), ch6.

death and suffering of war was witnessing an exhausted horse drop dead.

Once assigned to the supply lines, it was especially mules he worked with. They were very important, in spite of their reputed bad temperament. Mules were ideally suited, being more able to cope with the rough conditions and terrain than horses. But, as his diary reveals, they could eat through ropes and be difficult to control, and were a constant source of frustration and humour for troops,[71] although Philip mainly found them to be a test of his character! Unfortunately his diary ends soon after this period in early 1918. His military record shows that on 28th August, in the summer of that year, he was granted class 1 proficiency pay, which would have entailed passing certain tests.[72] During this time his company had been in "Samaria" reaching northwards towards Damascus and had not gone with the other troops east into Jordan, although, from the end of the diary in early 1918 until October, the 181st Heavy Artillery Battery continued to assist fighting, and especially "fleeing targets" at Kalkilieh, Hableh and Mulebbis and the Hableh Road to Rafat. The 95th H.A.G. Digest noted that May 1918 was a critical period in which artillery was of crucial assistance to advancing troops.[73] The extent of his journey is only hinted at by the reference to "in Samaria" in his contents list, and no further details are in his military record, but there was some heavy fighting, since his own Battery experienced casualties and deaths in this period.[74] The 181st were finally assigned to the coastal defences based at Haifa.[75] The remaining defensive responsibilities of his company meant they were not part of the final movement of troops that defeated the Turks in the North and East of the region. That part of the campaign had been accomplished quite rapidly from the end of 1917, with the Allied forces defeating the Turks at Megiddo on September 19th 1918, followed by Damascus and

---

71 Animals in WWI are described at www.firstworldwar.com/features/forgottenarmy.htm. See also *Mr Punch's History of the Great War* which includes references to the mule: www.gutenberg.org/files/11571/11571-h/11571-h.htm. The family remember a now missing photograph of Philip in uniform standing beside a mule.

72 Some of the skills included drill at guns, knotting and using ropes, use of jacks, drill in moving ordnance, nomenclature of stores etc. Walter B. Caddell, *Handbook for Proficiency Pay, Royal Garrison Artillery* (London: William Clowes and Sons, 1912).

73 The 181st Heavy Artillery netralised 6 enemy batteries and destroyed one completely. *H.A.G Digest 181st Heavy Battery,* The Royal Artillery Museum, Royal Arsenal, Woolwich, London, SE18 6ST.

74 May to August 1918 *H.A.G Digest* op.cit.

75 Ibid.

then, within a week, Sidon, Tyre and Beirut had surrendered, with Aleppo finally surrendering on October 26th. At the end of October, the Turks admitted defeat and signed an armistice at Mudros, on the island of Lemnos in the Aegean. The fast advance of this stage meant artillery played a much smaller role.

The post-armistice months were very difficult for British soldiers who were reluctant to remain when others closer to home were returning more quickly. As well as having been away from loved ones, there were anxieties about being last in the queue for civilian jobs. General Allenby increased the rate of men returning home since there was growing unrest, with the commendation that it had been a

> *"long campaign with a worthy foe, a test of endurance and stamina almost unequalled in the service of the crown."*[76]

Eventually, on 17th February 1919, Philip was sent back to Egypt, and, passing his medical examination in Ismalia, was allowed to return home. He departed from Port Said in Egypt on the S.S. Caledonia[77] arriving home on 4th March 1919. Although his diary does not cover this time, there is a vivid detail, albeit sentimental, regarding his return home from my Grandmother's recollection who remembered him saying that he was so moved by the sight of the green beauty of the British countryside that he shed a tear when first seeing it again.

He was demobilised on 2nd April at Dover and, along with all who had served in the war, received the British War Medal for entering the theatre of war, and the Victory Medal for being mobilised in active service.[78] His military records, from both periods of service, in India and in WWI describe his conduct and character as exemplary.

---

76 David Woodward, *Forgotten Soldiers of the First World War* (Stroud: Tempus, 2007), p278.

77 There was an SS Caledonia operating in the Mediterranean which was sunk in 1916, so this would have been the SS Caledonia that was a passenger mail ship between India and England, naturally passing Egypt through the Suez Canal. The ship was probably requisitioned for transport. An interesting note for the family is found in the picture at www.swanhellenic.com/library/ss-caledonia-13661.html and a description of a half-model that was viewable on board the *Minerva* cruise ships. Barbara, Philip's daughter enjoyed cruises on *Minerva* later in life, but would probably not have realised she was looking at a model of the ship on which her father travelled home.

78 These two medals, when worn together were nicknamed "Mutt and Jeff."

British War Medal and Victory Medal. Philip Bryant's name, service number and unit are inscribed on the side.

Reverse side of Philip Bryant's Victory Medal

Yorkshire to Devon

Once he left the army, he was able to return home. Millie and Philip settled into village life in York, and had two children – Barbara in 1920 and John in 1922. It is especially notable that a favourite mule under his care in the war was called Barbara, and it is said that this is where his daughter's name had come from![79]

Although he had worked as a commercial clerk before the war, and possibly for some time afterwards, he and Millie purchased the village grocery shop in Haxby which became their livelihood for many years. A memory of "Bryant's shop" is recorded in John T Wright's memoir of life as an evacuee in the second world war and gives a lovely detailed snapshot of the shop and its owners at that time:

> "Just past the school, there were three old, two-storey, terraced houses with grey tiled roofs and next to them was a grocer's shop with a red pantiled roof. A hand-painted sign on the board above its window declared 'P Bryant and Son' and Mrs Harris said to Archie, "The Bryant's [sic] son, John, is just a teenager but he helps out in the shop and his sister, Barbara, is your Harry's age." At the back of the shop, the small post office had a wooden counter with a wire mesh screen above it, which stocked everything from postage stamps to sealing wax. Posters and signs indicated that it sold Waverley pens; packets of nibs; lead pencils; crayons; Stephens' ink; blotting pads; boxes of chalk; notebooks and many other associated materials and it was here that the boys handed over their postcards to Mrs Mary [sic] Bryant, to be sent home. It was the only means of letting their parents know where they were billeted and, in the event of postcards being lost in transit or not posted at all, the local billeting officer sent the names and addresses of all evacuees to the relevant authorities who informed their schools."

---

79 Barbara was also a popular name in the Artillery, since Saint Barbara was their patron saint, with a feast day on 4th December, the day before Philip's birthday, but as a Nonconformist he may not have paid much attention to patron saints.

"The main part of the shop was a general dealers and grocers with signs advertising such mouth-watering things as Sharp's Kreamy Toffee, Huntley and Palmer's Biscuits, Tate and Lyle's Golden Syrup and Heinz Tomato Soup. It even stocked Veritas asbestos gas mantles, which were still being used in many of the local farms and cottages. A large red, black and white, tin sign adorned the front of the shop under the window, proclaiming "Smoke Craven A for your Throat's Sake" and a very tall man with a deep voice was serving. He was wearing a blue and white striped apron and had salt-and-pepper hair cut in a crew-cut style, which the boys thought looked like a steel-wool scouring pad. Mrs Harris said, 'That's Philip Bryant, the shop owner who lives in the two rooms upstairs with his wife and son. They bought the shop from the Wardles not long before the war started.'"[80]

The sweet (grocery) shop had stuck in John Wright's recollection, as might be expected of a small boy away from home in war years, but he also reveals a passing insight into the ethos of the Bryants:

"...we went to Bryant's for our sweets. Mrs Bryant, a big upright sort of woman, was not so fussy if our sweets weighed a little more than our few coppers justified, and she always put them in a conical-shaped paper bag, twisted at the top to close it."[81]

Outside of his work, local Methodist records demonstrate Philip also had a special enthusiasm for the Methodist Guild activities in Haxby, and served on various Methodist committees.[82] He occasionally preached, sometimes standing by with a sermon in case a preacher did not turn up, and in the 1930s would often take his daughter Barbara ready to play the organ when he led a service.

---

80 John T. Wright, *An Evacuee's Story a North Yorkshire Family in Wartime* (Harbury Warwickshire: Lulu.com, 2007), pp87-89.
81 Wright (2007) op.cit. p.287.
82 In the Wesleyan Guild he was, at various times, the social and musical secretary, often suggesting speakers for their festivals, devotional secretary, and general secretary. He spent a number of years as the President of the literary committee. The church belonged to the York and Clifton Circuit, and Philip served on the Foreign Missions committee there and other committees, a role which continued after moving to Devon.

Barbara graduated from Sheffield University with a special interest in French and music, and married a medical student, Desmond Greaves, in Haxby in July 1945. Her brother John moved to Devon, to work for the Royal Mail, then later as a taxi driver and finally as a watchmaker. John had poor health from respiratory problems as a result of childhood tuberculosis, so in 1949, just a few years after the Second World War, Millie and Philip moved to be near him at Beaford in Devon to run the village shop and Post Office there.

Philip continued to play an active part among the Methodists at Beaford. Zion chapel was originally part of the Bible Christian Church fellowship, a local denomination that amalgamated with the Methodists in the Hatherleigh circuit. The chapel still retains its original simple layout, with the words "He is faithful that promises" in capitals on the wall above the pulpit. In 1951, there were approximately fifty worshippers, and although he no longer preached, "Mr Bryant" is mentioned on the circuit plans as a Society Representative for the church, and attended quarterly circuit meetings, until they moved to Sidmouth in the spring of 1959. Towards the end of 1958, minutes of these meetings made reference to John's increased times of illness and sent greetings and letters of concern to Millie and Philip for which he was appreciative.

In his later years, Philip Bryant remained a formal, and outwardly austere person, characterised by his military background and strong religious convictions, but locally they were remembered as a quiet couple who loved gardening, growing vegetables, and playing cribbage. John was remembered for his wonderful sense of humour! Retiring to Sidmouth, they lived at Chyngton, 4 Primley Road where Philip died on the 30th May 1963 at the age of 81, with his family around him. His daughter, Barbara, vividly recalled his final words: "Lord, I come." His body was cremated at Torquay on 4th June.

Millie continued to care for her son John until she died in 1970. During that time, a niece made regular visits to be of assistance to John. Joan Bryant, whose father, Jesse, was Philip's younger brother, was from North West London since childhood, but later moved down to Exeter. Her help towards John, who died in 1975 was of immense value and a cause for much gratitude within the family. The ashes of Millie and her son John were interred in an unknown part of Sidmouth Cemetery.

This biographical sketch is intended to trace some of the historical details of Philip's life and background. As such, it can be seen that his life very much centred around his faith, his work and his family. In old age he was a somewhat formal and distant character, so his diary conveys a rare insight into the thoughts and feelings from his younger days, which were partly kept from others in later years.

As readers examine the diary, it should be noted that it has been transcribed as written with no alterations to spelling or grammar. The only alteration was to extract the "preface" as he called it, in order to place it at the front of the diary. As previously mentioned, footnotes have also been included wherever the transcriber felt the need to research a particular point, in the hope it would be of assistance to other readers. Philip Bryant may have felt a little surprise at the wider interest in his diary, but his thoughts and insights are now available for readers of generations to come, as well as members of his own family.

60 pounder heavy artillery gun of the kind used by Philip Bryant. Image from *The Handbook of Artillery* (1920), Washington: Government Printing Office, p189.

Action photograph of gunners firing a 60 pounder in Mesopotamia as Philip Bryant would have done in Egypt and Palestine.

The Great War Diary of Philip Bryant

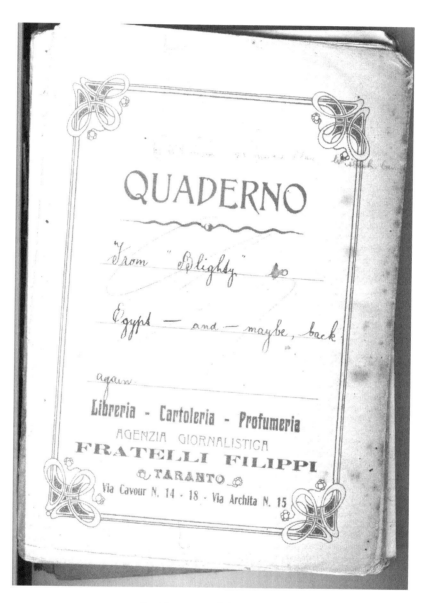

Inside cover of the Diary

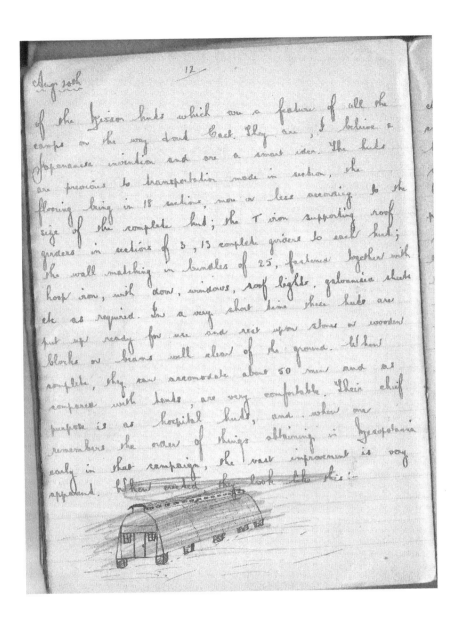

Aug 20th

12

of the prison huts which are a feature of all the camps on the way down East. They are, I believe a Japanese invention and are a smart idea. The huts are previous to transportation made in section, the flooring being in 18 section, more or less answering to the size of the complete hut; the T iron supporting roof girders in sections of 3, 13 complete girders to each hut; the wall matching in bundles of 25, fastened together with hoop iron, with door, windows, roof lights, galvanised sheets etc as required. In a very short time these huts are put up ready for use and rest upon stones or wooden blocks or beams well clear of the ground. When complete, they can accommodate about 50 men and as compared with tents, are very comfortable. Their chief purpose is as hospital huts, and when one remembers the order of things obtaining in Mesopotamia early in that campaign, the vast improvement is very apparent. When erected they look like this:—

Diary page

49

Philip Bryant.

"From Blighty to Egypt – and - maybe, back again."

---

[83] A section of part 4, and parts 5 and 6 are in a lost volume.

Preface [written in the middle of August 23rd 1917]

I make no pretence as a scribe, and am fully conscious of my literary limitations. The following record is written with a sense of obligation and with a fourfold purpose. I owe it to those who shall read it, as an expression of gratitude for their prayerful and loyally kind interest, to let them know how I fared as a soldier in Palestine. I write for the wife whose unfailing courage, cheerfulness, and unceasing prayerfulness has been under God the chief factor in keeping me cheerful and perseverant [sic] under trying conditions; for those friends whose practical worth has been revealed in so many ways to the help of both Mrs Bryant and myself; for my mother and all home folk including those in York, who always had me in remembrance, but primarily to the glory of God Whose loving care, gracious providence, and tender longsufference with my very many failings has made such a record as the following possible. A somewhat changing life up to the time I enlisted has a wonderful record of His mercies "ever faithful, ever sure,"[84] but I never was so conscious of my standing in Jesus Christ, or so sure of God's interest in me and mine as now. Perforce living under conditions uncongenial, and amid circumstances oft times very depressing, I have often fled to My Refuge, never to be disappointed or sent empty away; and it is in perfect sincerity and humble gratitude that I here record that but for my knowledge of Him, and His mindfulness of me, I should have gone the way of all mere flesh, lived as a beast,[85] and have only a past regret to record. Like Paul I would say "By the grace of God I am what I am",[86] and further add "God hath done great things for me whereof I am glad"[87] – and thankful.

---

84 Hymn: *Let us with a gladsome mind,* John Milton 1623.
85 Daniel 4:24-37 describes the madness of Nebuchadnezzar king of Babylon.
86 1 Corinthians 15:10.
87 Psalm 126:3.

Part 1 The Journey Out

Aug 17th 1916[88]

That which we - Millie & I - expected, has happened, and I am now for overseas service. This record of what I saw, thoughts and experiences on my journey from England to Egypt should fitly commence with a testimony of praise to God for answered prayer. On arrival at Winchester, my last station in England, I readily appreciated the fact that my next move would be overseas, and that that may take place very soon, and most probably to France. Now I "funked" France for two reasons. Firstly, I dreaded the awful pandemonium of noise. Since the break-down in India, I have been the harassed possessor of "nerves", and prolonged noise of even small volume becomes an agony. At Haile Sands Ford previous to going to Winchester, I was driven nearly frantic with the acute nervous agony caused by the noise made by workmen at work there, and that was really the cause of the haunting dread of the gun-fire in France. After my sojourn in India, I am too thin-blooded to be able to withstand cold unless protected by just those comforts missing out of an army life. The last winter at Spurn nearly "crocked" me. Under the circumstances, I felt quite justified in making this the matter of prayer, praying especially that I may be sent back, even to Mesopotamia, rather than be exposed to a winter in France. To my prayers were added the prayers of Millie, on whom I have come to rely as a prayer-warrior, and this record is the evidence in writing of the answer that God so graciously & wonderfully vouchsafed, so adding to the long long chain of evidence that He watches over me, over-ruling in everything for my good, and honouring the prayer-ministry of a wife whose prayers on my behalf are unceasing.

---

88 His Military record shows that this is the date he was actually conscripted. It was another year until he was sent to the Egypt Expeditionary Force. A year passes before the next entry of August 18th 1917.

Aug 18th

I, and seven other N.C.Os[89] had been under orders for an Eastern draft for about a fortnight when the order came suddenly on the evening of August 17th '17 to be ready to leave the following morning. Accordingly, on Saturday morning the 18th we paraded at 9 am outside our Company Office where we received pay in advance for five weeks and signed various documents. Our dress was service serge[90] and solar helmets, with equipment. After inspection by our O.C.[91] we were marched to the Brigade Office where other drafts were mustered and mustering for a final inspection and good-bye remarks by the Colonel Commanding. My feelings were rather mixed, for in addition to the natural excitement, I felt sorry to be leaving behind so many of the lads with whom I had been for so long. I felt also a qualm of anxiety regarding Millie, but with regard to this latter, I was re-assured by the sense of the Father's protecting and comforting power. My hand and arm ached after receiving the farewell from the boys. Headed by the brass and pipe bands of the London Irish, we left Morn Hill Camp at 11.15. One of the tunes played was "Take me back to dear old Blighty" ! ! ! After proceeding about a mile, I was detailed off to go ahead to the station and warn the R.T.O[92] of our approach, and on my way I called on Mr Stevenson of the Soldier's home, Winchester[93], and he came with me to the station. It was a hot day, and hurrying soon produced a heavy sweat, a foretaste of experiences to come. Mr S. very kindly treated me to a tin of Café au lait, chocolate and a welcome cup of tea. We had only a short wait for the troop train. I was delighted to get a hand shake from Miss Hobson (another Soldier's Home treasure) who put in an appearance just before the train moved off. In addition to our draft of 150 gunners and drivers, there were also

---

89 Non Commissioned Officers.
90 A type of fabric.
91 Officer Commanding.
92 Rail Transportation Officer. Responsible for the route and organisation of military trains.
93 There is a helpful insight into the origins of Winchester Soldier's Homes in R. Hall, *Things are Different now* (Winchester: Winchester Famiily Church, 2008) p.8-23.

infantry drafts. To the tune of "Auld lang syne" & cheers from onlookers, our train steamed out at 12 noon for Southampton Docks where we arrived after a run of a bout 20 minutes. En route, we picked up more troops. By a cheering coincidence, we dis-entrained on the same dock platform I arrived at on my return from India. A happy augury? After having lined up in drafts and removed our equipment, we were then told that we should have a wait of 5 hrs. This afforded us time to look around the docks, write letters etc. I wrote to Millie & then had a look around. The most interesting sight was the "aft-sunk" leviathan, the "Acquilania" lying at anchor in dock mid-stream. She has been rigged up as a hospital ship, but owing to her unwieldy size and the submarine menace, is now, out of service. It was a fine sight however and a wonderful example of man's ingenuity and power. Many of the troops were engaged in gambling, especially "Crown & Anchor", and from subsequent overheard remarks, not a few lost the larger part of their advanced pay. One really wonders why the authorities are not more strict in the matter of gambling, for so many of the lads have to be protected against themselves, and a "broke" soldier is invariably a discontented, & so a bad soldier. The happenings of interest did not prevent a "blueish" feeling, and I longed for home already! But God granted a grace upon my faint endeavour to keep smiling, and I managed to keep moderately cheerful. During the afternoon, troops of all regiments kept arriving until the platform became crowded. We fell in again about 6 pm and then proceeded to embark on the "Queen Alexandra", a turbine steamer previously on the Clyde River service. On boarding, every person was issued with a life - belt which was worn during the whole of the journey to Cherbourg. During the time of awaiting departure, the lads sang songs and gave the impression that we were all off on a picnic. A crowd of people outside the gate at the end of the basin cheered & waved handkerchiefs at intervals, compliments which were vigorously returned by the troops. Almost punctually at 8 o'clock we cast off & steamed away. There was a fascination in watching the distance between the boat and the dock side - England - widen from inches to feet and then to yards, hundreds of yards & so on until the steamer was under full steam ahead. Somehow a lightness in the throat would, in spite of all attempts at preocution,[94] keep occurring, and the question "where to ?" & "When returning ?" suggestively arose. It was a glorious evening, and the passage down the beautiful Southampton Water, past Hythe & on to the Solent was delightful. We were able to pick out Cowes, Hyde & Yarmouth as we passed from West to East, North of the I. of Wight. By the time we got abreast of Portsmouth Harbour, all the fort searchlights were playing, and presented a magnificent spectacle. Before we were well clear of the Island, we were all ordered below decks, so as to ensure no light from striking matches etc. And no noise being heard and seen during the night passage. Then began the discomforts. We were heavily laden, and the deck space below didn't permit all the troops to get laid down; for part of this space was taken up with kits etc. As there was no sleeping accommodation, it meant that we had to get settled down as best we could. I foresaw the difficulty, and early ensconced myself on a bag, and pile of equipment, an uncomfortable bed, but by no means the worst available. It had one very big advantage, and that was, that it was clear of the deck, and far enough removed from possible places where second hand meals were likely to be shot. This interesting practice soon started, for although the passage across the Channel was good, there was sufficient roll to cause mal-de-mer among several of the Tommies. The demonalic tendencies of Father Neptune asserted themselves during the whole run across, several obeyed his policy of "Up with everything that's down". There were no means of ejecting in suitable places, the only spots where this could be done being very early filled with squads of suffering soldiery, so the others, perforce had to unship their cargoes where they could with the least inconvenience to the rest of the passengers. In a very short time, the decks were inaccessible. But for a sense of humour, and a spirit of cheerfulness, the passage would have a been a nightmare. Fortunately, I kept A.1. No sound sleep was possible, for in addition to the character of the bed, the sound of the efforts of the sick men kept one

---

94 Prequit: to stop doing it before you start.

awake. One of the lads, an H.L.I.[95] man, apparently gave up the attempt to get to sleep, and forthwith began to slit the atmosphere with mouth organ solos and the singing of patter songs.[96] I managed to doze fitfully as soon as our Scotch harmonist got tired, but awoke again at 2 a.m. as the engines reversed and finally stopped. We were at Cherbourg after a run of about 6 hrs. I slept again until dawn was just breaking and soon was able to get a view of the harbour.

Aug 19th

The harbour itself is unattractive, but the environment of hills add a touch of prettiness to an otherwise ordinary scene. We "inched" our way to the dock side and soon after our arrival there, was met by a torpedo-boat destroyer, which had escorted us across, and which also carried a draft of sailors for the East. We disembarked about 8.30 am and lined up in drafts on an open space near by. After sundry preliminaries, we were then marched off to a rest camp. The tramp through Cherbourg was very interesting. The houses, although old for the most part, were very quaint and in many cases pretty, bordered as they were by gardens with flowers, chiefly asters, growing in profusion. A noticeable feature was the cordial attitude of the people, especially the older folk, many of the old dames bowing and the old grand-dads raising their hats as we passed. The boys sang with vigour as they marched, some happily inspired chorister starting "Tipperary" to the apparent delight of the townspeople among whom "Tipperary" must have become very familiar. It was a hot morning and we soon got very warm. Fortunately we had left our kits on the wharf - side in charge of a black labour squad for package in the train that was to take us to Italy. The latter part of our four mile march was through glorious country reminiscent of the Yorkshire Wolds, and on the way we passed a chalet in a beautiful situation which had been converted for the use of the hospital authorities for

---

95 Highland Light Infantry.
96 Used in comic opera and musicals.

wounded officers. On arrival at the camp we breakfasted off biscuits, cheese & marmalade, an "elegant" Sunday morning breakfast.

We found on our arrival at camp that we should be confined there until 6 p.m. the following day. There was sufficient of interest however to keep us amused, one of the features being the work of the black (West Indian) labour squad. I shall have more to write about them later.[97] No provision for a service had been made so I got aside and had a good read, prayer & meditation. A rumour got abroad that a German submarine was sunk outside the harbour during the night. I cannot vouch for the truth of it, but the rumour was productive in me of a sense of reassurance that I am in the safe keeping of Him who has my name engraved on the palm of His hand. During the evening I got a little "blueish" and thought wistfully of home, and the Soldier's Welcome at Winchester where I knew I was prayed for. It gives one tremendous confidence when they know that such a power of prayer is exercised by so many on his behalf. I rejoice in the fact that my last Sunday in Blighty was so grand and memorable. We slept 10 in a tent so hadn't any room to spare. I kept warm until about 3.30 am & then awakened shivering, for it had turned desperately cold. Others were also awake, and they met the situation by singing songs. The spirits of some is a thing beyond comprehension, but appears to be a striking characteristic of the British Tommy who will sing & joke amid the most depressing conditions and circumstances. I "snuggled" up to a corporal and dropped off to sleep again, and heard nothing more until reveille sounded. I was rather stiff after sleeping on the bare ground.

Aug 20th

Here in the camp I had my first sight of the Nissan huts which are a feature of all the camps on the way & out East. They are, I believe a Japanese invention and are a smart idea. The

---

97 Apart from a brief further reference on August 22nd, this is probably in the lost volume.

huts are, previous to transportation, made in section, the flooring being in 18 sections, more or less according to the size of the complete hut; the T iron supporting roof girders in sections of 3, 13 complete girders to each hut; the wall matching in bundles of 25, fastened together with hoop iron, with door, windows, roof lights, galvanised sheets etc. as required. In a very short time these huts are put up ready for use and rest upon stones or wooden blocks or beams well clear of the ground. When complete, they can accommodate about 50 men and as compared with tents, are very comfortable. Their chief purpose is as hospital huts, and when one remembers the order of things obtaining in Mesopotamia early in that campaign, the vast improvement is very apparent. When erected, they look like this: -

[DIAGRAM - although he then tried to scribble it out with pencil.]
    After tea, we paraded for departure at 6.00 pm & left camp at 6.15 pm. Previous to moving off, the Camp Commandant gave a very suitable address to the assembled troops, quite an unexpected feature. Our march back to the docks was just one long pleasure jaunt. Some fun was caused by the efforts of some of the men to purchase goods, especially bread through the medium of sundry boys who ran alongside the marching troops. Occasionally, the boy returning with the purchases couldn't find the purchaser, and the goods were promptly sequestrated by others. En route, flowers, especially asters, were distributed by the people, and in a very short time, most of the lads had their helmets and rifles etc. decorated. Some of these rifles by the way, were carried by youngsters, who were delighted with what they no doubt felt to be our honour. Singing & cheering was the general order, and every little untoward incident such as when a cart, driven by a very pretty & very embarrassed young lady ran into a refuse cart, was seized upon as worth a roar of laughter and an avalanche of jokes. One result of the boisterous good humour was that few, if any thought of wither past or future. Certainly, I didn't. That came later. Arriving at the docks, we found our train drawn up ready for boarding. We were arranged six in a compartment and on the whole were

comfortable. Some of the troops travelled 1st Class, some 2nd, and others 3rd. The 3rd class are a long way removed in comfort from those at home, for the one I travelled in had hard springless cushioned seats, but plain board backs. One compensating feature however was, that all we "Y" Battery NCOs travelled together. We had a wait of about an hour & a half before we moved off, but it was by no means a weary wait, for the boys sang songs continuously to the delight of several French soldiers from a barracks near by. Again "Tipperary" was a well known & general favourite with the natives. Rather a funny incident occurred when one French poilu[98] who had been to London & picked up a smattering of English, asked us to sing certain songs. He didn't know the names of them so he hummed each chorus in turn, which choruses included "Keep the home fires burning", "Who's your lady friend", "Tennisee" etc. The lads delightedly obliged in full-throated unison. Some happily inspired Tommy then started the Marseillaise. Few if any of us knew the complete wording, but everybody "la-da-d" until they got to the words "March on", and then ripped out with a gusto. The effect was comically great on the French-people civilian & soldier alike, for in response, they clapped & cheered with a great will. Someone remarked "If they carry on like this now, what will they be like when we return?" There wasn't a quiet moment anywhere right up to the time of our departure at 9.20 pm, when the yells, cheers & shouts of civilian and soldier alike will, I guess, never be forgotten by our men at any rate. So commenced our long train journey towards the land of the Pharaohs.

We travelled East for a while, through the Province of Manche (my map was a French one, so that the names given will be in the majority of cases, the French form of the word) and before turning in to sleep, stopped at Valognes. During the night we passed through Caen Bayeaux and Alencon. I was awake at these places for I had a big job to get settled down after the excitement of a few hours previous, and also owing to the nature of the bed. We passed out of Manche, and through

---

98 A French word, meaning "shaggy" or "hairy" used to describe infantrymen in
WWI of humble backgrounds with bushy beards or moustaches.

the Province of Calvados during the darkness, and awoke in the morning as we entered the Lorne Province. We were not travelling very fast, a fact which we all hoped would obtain until we got to our journey's end, for everybody was keen to see as much as possible during the travel.

August 21st

A closed truck was attached to the rear of the train in which the rations for the whole train for the complete journey was packed but we stopped at intervals for breakfast and tea, and incidentally for ablutions, at appointed rest halls. The first of these was at a wayside station, Columbiers, which we arrived at at 7.45 a.m. The arrangements here, as at nearly all other such places were very decent. Telegraphic notification had been sent ahead, and on our arrival, hot water, ready for making tea was awaiting us. After breakfast, a wash and the issue of rations for the day, we resumed our journey. Our first important stopping place after this resumption was at the big manufacturing town of Le Mans at which place we arrived at 10.30 a.m. We halted there for about half an hour and I seized the opportunity to purchase a card and send it to Millie. A chat with some war veteran French soldiers was interesting though difficult, for our French and their English were very elementary. But mutual interest and desire enabled us to get along fairly well. They wouldn't say much about their experiences, but with these men, as with all other French people whom we spoke to here and elsewhere there was no possibility of doubt re their hatred of the Boche and their desire to fight him to a complete finish, to smash him. We passed though beautiful county after this, and stopped at several wayside stations, at each of which there was a group of country people, very kind and generous in their distribution of fruit and flowers. One little lad was so carried away by his feelings that not content with a gift of a big basket full of apples and pears, he distributed the few 10 centine pieces he had in his pockets. Perhaps needless to add, our men gave him English pennies in exchange. This however was quite unexpected by him and at first he declined them.

We were now passing through the beautiful district of Sarthe of which province Le Mans is a town. Although men of military age, not in uniform were very rarely seen, the country side appeared fully cultivated, the crops being the same as in England. At one station, Eccommoy, a lad distributed small photos of himself with a request in queens English that the recipient would write to him. I got one, and I shall certainly write to him as soon as I get a settled address for him to write to. It was a glorious day, and everybody was enjoying the trip immensely. To me, the panorama and the interesting incidents kept me on the qui vive[99] the whole day long. The train travelled slowly and this was a great treat, for it gave us plenty of time to observe things. As we progressed, we ran into a great fruit growing country, the trees being positively weighted down with fruit. During the day, I had a very strengthening, and peace-giving sense of God's care for me. I felt grateful for an appreciative eye and spirit that could enjoy at its real value, the beauties of nature.

Passing out of Sarche, into the Province of Indre et Loire, we passed through the town of Mettray, and arrived at a halt on the outskirts of Tours at 4.30. The halt was very welcome, for although I experienced nothing in the nature of train fatigue, the opportunity for a walk, a wash and a drink of tea came as a relief. We could see little of the town as a whole, although what we could see gave the impression that it was a very fine city. The outskirts were very pretty and consisted for the main part of fruit orchards and market gardens. I would have paid most any price for a descriptive guide, such as a Baedakers for it would have multiplied the interest greatly. After a two hour wait, we left at 6.30; and almost immediately began to run through a different sort of country. The change was remarkable. The cultivation of the vine was more general here, and we passed several pretty vineyards. Soon after leaving

---

99 Fr. lit. "Long live who?"used as a sentry's challenge meaning "Whose side are you on?" Philip used the term here meaning to be on the alert.

Tours, we had a journey through a piece of wonderful scenery. On one side of the railway, we skirted the Cher River for several miles and the gradually softening light of day was reflected in the water in ever changing colours, the direct effect of the vari-coloured vegetation. As a contrast, on the other side of the line, huge rocks and cliffs seemed to leap up into the sky, so steep and sheer were they. The cliffs were honeycombed with rock dwellings and wine cellars, a quaint and pretty effect. One huge rock with a dwelling hewed into it was very suggestive of "The Rock of Ages" and I had a new conception of the Rock as a defence, a dwelling-place and an object of beauty. At this point, as far as I could see, every window was crowded with men, the doors of the carriages in the majority of carriages being open, the footboards being occupied by men sitting and standing., Nowadays, one reads and hears much of the versatile powers of the English Tommies, but they have today given a wonderful demonstration of both their high spirits and their astonishing endurance of lung power. All day today they have cheered almost continuously, even individual kiddies, so long as they waved in reply, being cheered in unison. Where groups were gathered when at stations or at intervals between, French compliments were hurled at them and sounds of cheers.

At a little wayside station, St Aignon-le-Moyers, some French Red - or to be literally correct - Rouge Croix nurses served out weak aniseed water to the train. We got this at other places along the route and apparently it is a feature of troop train arrangements throughout France. I am not sufficiently expert in medicinal affairs to state the good properties of this drink, but it was pleasant, and certainly better than aqua pura. Also, at this station, we were again the recipients of fruit and flowers. Already we have been convinced of the generous hospitality and whole-hearted welcome of the French people toward the British soldier, and anticipate good times further along. At this station, (St Aignan-le-Moyers) the donors were drawn from all sections, and included the fashionably dressed and the poorest garbed from the community. Some of the girls, about 16 years of age, flirted with some of our youngsters, who, to the gleeful delight of the civilian onlookers, and those affected, kissed their pretty companions as the train moved off.

By this time (nearly nightfall) the train was festooned with flowers and covered with complimentary phrases in - more or less - French. On our carriage we had chalked "Viva le Francaise"!! It was subsequently altered to the correct form.

It has been a wonderful day, this. From daybreak to sunset has been one long pleasure jaunt, with scarcely a moment that wasn't full of interest and novelty. I had a sense of gratitude to God, and "warmed" to my devotions which were practised in the "toilette". In spite of the character of the prayer chamber, I felt very near to God and had a grand half an hour.

About 10.30 p.m. we ran into a big junction Vierzon, in the Province of Loire-et-Cher and waited in a siding until we moved off again at 2 a.m. Few of the men turned in until we resumed the journey, the line side being dotted with groups of chaps, chatting or singing songs. I sat up also.

August 22nd

I had a good sleep and awoke at 6.15 am, The scenery hereabouts was not so interesting and for some time, nothing of unusual interest was seen. After passing through Nevers (during the early morning) in Nievre Province, and Moulins a big town in the Province of Allier, we arrived at a little place, Paray-le-Monial in the Province of Saône et Loire at 7.40 a.m. and halted for breakfast etc. We were now about 80 miles off Lyons. There, I would add a reference to the excellent medical arrangements made for the convenience of the troops travelling. At short intervals along the route there were medical rooms, and if at any point, a man had fallen sick, he would have had a very short wait before receiving medical attention. In addition to this, British medical officers travelled with the train. We had a long wait at P. le Monial and didn't leave again until 12.55 after a wait of 4 ¼ hrs. After leaving here, the scenery became increasingly pretty and interesting, the character of the country being pastoral. Progressing through le Clayette we then passed into the Rhône Province, and shortly afterwards, the railway ran along the top of a high ridge from which, for miles, we had a grand view of the undulating landscape on either side. Evidently, this is a favourite residential district for the well-to-do for the countryside is dotted with fine châteaux. Occasionally, we passed remains of abbeys & castles which reminded me of books I had read where the scenes were laid in medieval France. The houses too are very pretty in these parts and give additional colour to the view.

The troops were now scattered all over the train like so many monkeys, some of them climbing up the steps at the ends of the carriages and riding on top, and all along the footboards. The stops were frequent, acceptable, and apparently a part of the arrangements, for each stop was of say more than 5 minutes duration, which allowed the troops to get out and stretch their legs a bit.

On either side, the countryside developed into deep valleys, a magnificent panorama, and one bridge over which we ran was fully ¾ mile long and 300 feet high, a fine engineering feat. In the distance to the north, mountains could be seen. A very pretty touch of colour was given by the heather which grew in profusion. The last I saw growing was at Strensall!! Oh loh! Those thoughts of home. It needs but the faintest resemblance to anything homelike to send our thoughts winging Blighty-wards. In these parts we noticed that bullocks were commonly used for draught purposes, and frequently we saw those long, two big wheeled, wine casks one sees so often in the wine-merchants advertisements.

We now seemed to run off the ridge and during the afternoon, we were travelling almost along the centre of a beautiful valley. Huge forests on either side ran up the hill sides and as the sun sank lower, the shadow effect suggested a Master Hand at work on a bit of the most magnificent beauty I had ever seen.

About 2 p.m. we began to run through a series of short tunnels in the Belmont District at the end of each, revealing to us some fresh touch of glorious landscape. In contrast to the clean, bright countryside, the faces of those daring individuals who rode through the tunnels on the outside of the carriages appeared grotesque. The smoke from the engine blackened their faces to a degree when they were unrecognisable. Of course, this added to the gaiety of the others.

The religious character of the people was very evident in the fairly numerous shrines and images seen from the train. As a rule, the images, if apart from the shrines, stood on prominences, and one huge image of Christ stood on an isolated high rock facing the valley sloping downwards. However one may condemn and deplore the system and belief represented by these shrines and villages, there was something beautiful and spiritual about these marks of devotion, for the images at least, if not the shrines were probably placed in these positions out of love to God and of a desire for service toward the fellow countrymen of the donors. I felt too something of the irresistible appeal it must make to the devout Catholics, the sight of this magnificent image of the Lord with arms outstretched in entreaty to a world of suffering, sinful humanity.

The vineyards in these, the Chessay & Lozanne districts were the finest seen so far. They seemed to stretch for miles up the hill sides, the grapes being beautifully and most temptingly ripe and big. We did manage to get a few as we went along through the wayside stations. But, to me, the prettiest feature in nature of the day, were the little waterfalls and hill torrents we frequently passed. One spate seemed to rush down a cliff near the railway, along a ridge and then to leap out toward the train, only to fall short in its attempt, and to drop into a big pool by the line side. Whole villages and single houses were picturesquely perched on the top of the hills, each village, the possessor of a church, invariably a fine structure. In contrast however to the châteaux, plentifully strewn hereabouts as in the district passed earlier on, we passed groups of cottages which were picturesquely disreputable. I think the reason why the poverty was not so noticeable, as, for instance, some of the poorest houses passed yesterday, was because they appeared to be better built, this being undoubtedly due to the plentiful supply of building stone in the district. But a noticeable fact was, that even amongst the poorest of the poor, we never saw a single instance of shoe dirt and raggedness usually identified with similar poverty in England. Maybe this was due to the fact that the boys and girls were commonly clothed with an outside garment like a smock made from some black material. But even allowing for this, there still remains the fact of clean faces. I have read about the warm-hearted, generous French, and not one whit of all I have read that is good of their national traits has been exaggerated or overdrawn: at least, that is my impression after the perforce haphazard acquaintanceship I have made with them thus far.

About 5 p.m., we pulled up at Le Germain, a village 12 miles from Lyons, and we disembarked for our first long rest at the camp built near the line. We found the camp to be not nearly so nice and comfortable as that at Cherbourg, but taking everything into consideration, there was little to grumble about. The chance of a good splash was welcome, and in addition, I seized the opportunity to wash out some dirty "clobber". The "black" labour squads were very evident here, and were mostly engaged in building camp roads and erecting huts.

I turned into "bed" on boards with a feeling that I had again had a wonderful day. It is hard to separate the impressions and ideas formed, for every moment was fraught with unusual interest and impact. But the dominant idea running as a theme amid the others, is that of adoration to God for the marvellous work and beauty of His hands, for eyes to see them, and for senses to "taste" them, for that best expresses how the sights appealed to me.

August 23rd

I awoke on the morning of Thursday Aug 23rd feeling fit after a good night's rest in spite of the boards. Before going to sleep, I lay, and in the quietness had very helpful communion with the Friend. How grand a thing it is that He makes His presence felt at all times, and in any place, to those who diligently seek Him. What a grand plus is added to life when one can claim His friendship: what a wealth is added to one's joy of living to be able to say

"And so we live together,

My Friend and I..."

I think the general feeling of all our train party was that of a desire to be on the move again. The never-to-be-forgotten experiences of the last three days had sharpened our appetites for more, and we had great expectations of as great, if not greater pleasures to come. So with willing hearts, we paraded for re-entraining at 2 p.m. Some fun was got by the onlookers out of the figure cut by a draft of the Expeditionary Force Canteen section of the Army Service Corps who were travelling with us. Nearly all of these men were over 35 years of age, all of them being "C" category men, specially enlisted for service in the canteens, officers messes and clubs etc. at the bases and in the field and so affording release of men wanted for more serious work. For the most part, they were grocers etc. and about as unmilitary looking a gang as could be found anywhere. But they viewed their military standing as ipso facto, and did their best on and off parade to play the soldier correctly. Practically none of them had ever done a drill and their N.C.O.s were men without any military knowledge and given stripes probably according to their business standing. So that their efforts in a military direction were often ludicrous. Their attempt to "form forms" would have done credit to 'Fred Karnos'[100] troupe, and until they got more used to things, their

---

100 Fred Karno 26th March 1866 - 17th Sept 1941 was a popular music-hall show
    entertainer. Such entertainment was eventually replaced by the cinema. On the
    Western Front soldiers began to sing various versions of his theme tune 'We are
    Fred Karno's Army.'

appearance, a direct incentive to mirth, hilarious of course, on the part of the other troops. However, they were quite serious in their profession which they no doubt insisted was military, and persevered until eventually they proved, what has so often been proved in this war, that at the call of need, men can adapt themselves to the most undreamt of circumstances.

We left Le Germain about 3 p.m. and after a run of 45 minutes arrived at Lyons. As the station is built on a hill, we had a good view of the city and its environs. It appeared to be a very finely built place with splendid buildings standing out prominently. The station was liberally beflagged and here and there one detected the Union Jack and the flags of other Allied nationalities. Here where we halted for three quarters of an hour, we were given our first free issue of cigarettes, four packets per man. Later on I shall have more to say about this issue. We were also issued with the now famous M&V (meat and vegetable) ration consisting of meat, beans, carrots, potatoes, rice and peas all ready cooked and can be eaten cold or when heated hot. Of course, this issue was eaten cold, and really tasted fine. Apparently the station was a "closed" one, but that didn't prevent some of our lads holding a conversation – more or less intelligible – with sundry folk who were in the street below and communicable by means of a[101] railed in opening in the platform. Exchange of souvenirs were made, and many lads were subsequently short of jacket bullions, badges etc. We had a good send off at 4.30 p.m. Shortly after leaving Lyons, one of our draft fell off the footboard and was badly injured in addition to narrowly escaping death from a passing train. He was left on the lines, and not until about a month afterwards when he returned to us did we know what had really become of him. He was picked up and treated first at Lyons and then at St Germains.

At Amberieu and for about 30 miles onward, we met with a reception greater even than that previously experienced. In return, our lads showered cigarettes through the carriage windows, English Cigarettes being apparently specially

101 The Preface pages were here before the text continued.

acceptable, and in a very short time, the greater part of the cigarette issue had been distributed. We were now approaching the spurs of the Alps and the scenery wonderful beyond description. One mountain gorge through which we passed reminded me very much of the Nilghiris in S. India, rills madly rushing riverwards, woods in their grandeur softening the rugged tone of the landscape, roads and tracks lacing the whole together as though to prevent the falling asunder of the wonderful natural mosaic. High up on a huge solitary rock, reaching heavenwards was a huge crucifix. Ah yes, the emphasis of direction, even of the Cross is upward to God. This crucifix suggested the supremacy of the Cross, standing as it did so high and commanding. Really, I am after all something of a ritualist, for I felt profoundly impressed by this sight. Much as I object to any "aid" which tends to obscure the real Object of all true "worship", or which befogs the simple path of approach to God, I feel bound to recognise the value of such tangibilities to those whose minds and temperaments are such as to be humanly incapable of sensing God without such assistance, or who find in them the means of grace that I feel grateful I can do without. I remember too, that these things must have meant much indeed to Brother Lawrence,[102] Bernard of Clairvaux,[103] Thomas a Kempis,[104] and other saints of God through whom He has enriched the Christian world. Let me pray "Lord, make me very tolerant, very charitable."

I think we all had a feeling that each day had been more wonderful that its predecessors, for the scenery hereabouts was more arrestingly entrancing that any yet seen. Sombre peaks, sentinels of Nature; frowning cliffs stern reminders of the "awe" side of Nature; the rollicking happy-go-lucky, catch-me-if-you-can, spates of water; the softening, soothing forests; the still, calm restful valleys; "oh that men would praise

---

102 Brother Lawrence, 1614-1691, author of the Christian classic *The Practice of the Presence of God.*

103 Bernard of Clarivaux, 1090-1153, a monastic contemplative mystic, known for a number of works including *On Loving God* and for the words of the hymn *O Sacred Head Sore Wounded.*

104 Thomas a Kempis, 1380-1471, author of the Christian classic *The Imitation of Christ.*

the Lord for all His wonderful works." Some of the rocks leaped 500 feet sheer from the nail edge; gorges at other places lay as many feet below; valleys ran winding away to the horizon. Perched on a few cliffs one could discern statues of the Virgin, even the type of God's seal on the glory of ideal womanhood. The lacework of roads suggested that the road builders were artists as well as clever engineers. Queer houses here are built near the line, tall dwellings built on the flat system, anything but beautiful and rather suggestive of man's botch work as in contrast with the infinitely majestic handiwork of the Creator. But most of the girls were beautiful and generous in their distribution of "blown" kisses. And so we played hide and seek around hill and mountain, over stream and vale until when entering the province of Ain, we came to the River Loire again. By some trick of mentality, the boys in my carriage got to discussing the mad ambition of the Kaiser who would lay such a people as we have seen under the worst kind of tribute. We felt that we understood in part at least the wonderful "land love" of the French.

Arriving at Culoz we halted there for about an hour, and while there, a long train mostly filled with refugee children passed through, cheering frantically, and singing the stirring "Marsellaise". We seized the chance here, as elsewhere to augment our rations with purchases of bread, butter, tomatoes etc. As we progressed further, crowds lined the route and cheered, and you may be sure our lads didn't spare their lungs and throats. Sometimes the reception almost appeared ludicrous. In getting dark, we made arrangements for sleeping (I was now travelling First Class) and were just dozing off when cheering attracted us in a hurry to the windows when a remarkable sight rewarded us. We found ourselves entering a large town, and the roads running down to the railway were lined with youngsters armed with flaming torches, a very pretty effect. When we drew into the station, we found we were at Aix-le-Baines. Here was another big cheering crowd, several of whom waved Union Jacks. Perhaps here I ought to remark that troops trains going east had been passing this way for nearly two months, so it speaks well for the character of the enthusiasm of our French friends. It was no good trying to get to sleep after leaving A-le-B for we kept passing groups of cheering natives, some of whom we could see perched on the verandahs of the big dwelling houses. We arrived at Chambery, another fairly big station about 10 p.m. and here met another big cheering crowd, which in this case was largely composed of French soldiers. You might suppose that we were getting rather a surfeit of cheering, but not a bit of it. We yelled as enthusiastically and readily as ever before. A little further on we were side tracked at a small station, Magland for two hours where we had tea. Mark the hour. I rather fancy there had been some misarrangement regarding our time table. Anyhow, late as it was, the tea was both welcome and good. In fact, it was a distinct feature of the tea provided everywhere in France, that it was first class. On resuming our journey, we soon managed to "coil down" and get to sleep, and passing during the night through the passes of the French Alps awoke in the morning about 5.30 at Modane on the frontier between France and Italy.

Aug 24th

Here were the real Alps that one reads about. Snow capped, sun kissed mountains, the highest of which hereabouts is Mont Cenis [105]ft high. Oh I'll not attempt to describe the grandeur of it all. In fact, my impressions were rather too blessed to analyse. Wonderment; enchantment, awe, imagination, these were only some parts of the whole feeling. I am painfully conscious often of my very limited vocabulary, but rarely so as now when I try to describe these wonderful mountains. But what I cannot describe, I thank God I can feel. I am grateful for an impressionable mind and spirit. These high flung peaks remind me of their Creator Who is my God and Father. To me, they represented in some measure the strength of Him Whose eye turneth to and fro thought the whole earth, to show Himself strong on my behalf.[106] The hand that shaped

---

105 Should read 6827. A gap was left for later insertion.
106 2 Chronicles 6:9.

the Alps, guards me and mine. I wondered what the lad, a prodigal son, to whom I spoke last evening about his soul, thought. I didn't get a chance to ask him. Here again occurs the thought, He Whose might is seen in these rugged and yet perfectly harmonious (that's the word that best expresses the thought) heights condescended to use me and work through me for the good of a wayward lad of His.

Many of the mountains were magnificently cloaked with huge forests of firs running half way it seemed up their sides.

Modane is the terminus of this section of the French railway so we had to change into Italian railway carriages. Just a word about French railways as I saw them. They certainly do not attain to the British degree of comfort and speed. I surmise that being state owned and there being therefore no competition, there is not the inducement to provide luxurious travel. But on the whole, the French system we afterwards found is superior to the Italian.

We had a halt of nearly four hours and so after transferring our baggage etc., we looked around us at everything worth our inspection. We were not allowed far outside the gates and saw but little of the town; but perched right up the mountain side we could see the frontier fort garrisoned by the famous French Alpine Chasseurs[107] some of whom were on sentry near the station. An aerial railway ran from the fort to the main street below, and we saw supplies transported by this. Among other purchases, I bought some glorious butter at a farm for about three quarters of a pound.

I felt pleased and grateful that the lads with whom I travelled from St Germain - where I got separated from my Winchester chums - specially requested me to keep with them, and we managed to all get together in a 3rd class carriage a big change from that we vacated. It was a long open carriage with wooden uncushioned seats on either side of a central passage, which however undesirable otherwise, at least was airy, and afforded plenty of facilities for sight seeing. The engines, one in

---

107 The elite mountain infantry of the French army.

front and rear of the train, were electrically driven, and were Westinghouse engines of exactly the same type as those in use on the District Railway, London. Leaving Modane about 9.15 a.m., we almost immediately entered the Mt. Cenis tunnel which is hewn, or rather drilled through the mountain range for a distance of 12 miles. At intervals, where the tunnels ran near the mountain side, openings were cut affording snap glimpses of the outside scenery. So we came to the Italian frontier station of Bardonecchiatives. Here seemed in sharp contrast featurally with the French; rather surprisingly so, when one considered the short intervening distance between the two stations. Some beautiful Italian girls, of evident good social standing, distributed small buttonhole Italian flags, and picture post cards. I don't think I am even unduly impressed by a pretty face, or I might have "hung my hat up" elsewhere than I did in York, but I confess to an exceedingly lively interest in these dark eyed beauties. Picturesquely garbed, with their light olive complexions, perfectly clean, and merry, heart enslaving dark eyes, they enravished not a few of our lads, including this case-hardened, far-travelled, misanthrope. Of course, at my age, it did not fall to my good fortune to have my flag pinned to my shirt. They must have noticed the obvious that I am married. One lad suggested that God made the girls to match the scenery, not a bad surmise, and an apt compliment.

We had another glorious view of the range from here; in fact we could see longer stretches of the snow capped summits. Near the station was an Italian fort corresponding to that at Modane, but the Italian Alpine Corps were more picturesquely uniformed in blue grey tunics and breeches, stockings and shoes and a soft felt hat with a long eagle's feather jauntily set at an angle at the side. Leaving B. we ran through a series of short tunnels cut in the sides of the rocks, and at intervals when running in the open, we looked down sharp ridges anything up to 500 ft deep. The panorama was indescribably majestic. On the far side of the valley we could see waterfalls, some with sheer drops of several hundred feet, and silvery looking rills tracing patterns down the mountain sides. Some of the larger falls were harnessed for driving the machinery in factories that dotted the foot hills below. Somehow it struck me as rather presumptuous of man to so convert a natural wonder and joy to mundane use. Vandalism, I felt it to be. But there - I was born in London. Spurs of the Alps ran down towards the Plain of Piedmont and these were well covered near their bases with vineyards, which added considerably to the beauty of the landscape. Quite startlingly noticeable in contrast to the natural beauty around was the appearance of the natives who were dirty, ill clothed and indolent looking. The fairly numerous churches were invariably beautiful churches and one wondered if there were not some truth in an assertion that a priest ridden people is a poor people. Already we were conscious of a huge difference between France and Italy, a difference very favourable to the former. Further on in the Piedmont Valley, the soil, though clearly of the best, was only indifferently cultivated. The hill spurs were dotted beautifully with castles and mansions and appeared to be a sort of a Dukeries. We expected to pass through Turin, but to our disappointment we were run on to a loop line and so into a goods siding where we halted for two hours to allow the wheels and bearings to cool off after the run down from the mountains. Here we experienced our first real discomfort since leaving Cherbourg. It was hot, there was no water to be had for drinking or washing and our view consisted of trucks and wagons. It was felt to be a bad start of the journey through Italy. Ordinary locomotives were here attached, and we were glad when we recommenced our progress. In contrast again with what obtained in France, we either ran through stations, or when we halted, had no chance to fill our water bottles, and as the heat now was fairly powerful, we felt the lack of water. We also had an opportunity to rest our throats and lungs, for we passed no cheering crowds or parties here. Perhaps it is rather anticipating events to be recorded but here I may state that there seemed little, if any enthusiasm for the war in Italy. In fact, some English speaking Italian soldiers frankly told some of our lads that they didn't care for their job, and but for England, the war would have been over and they would be back in their homes. Of course, the Italians were soon in disfavour with our troops, signs of this becoming very apparent later.

We arrived at Asti, a big town about 7.30 p.m. where there was a guard of Bersaglieri[108] with their liberally befeathered hats. Apparently the Italian government were keeping this crack regiment up to pre-war standard, at least as regards physique, for they were a fine body of men we saw. By the way, the Italians were clearly not short of men, for every station we passed through had several troops on guard duty, and these, men of fighting grade. Then too, there seemed something significant in the fact that the railways everywhere were closely and heavily guarded. What were the authorities afraid of ? We were interested in noting the bullock carts drawn by bulls harnessed to a queer yoke with an attachment running overhead and straps fastened to the heads of the cattle apparently to keep their heads up, a similar thing to a bearing rein.

At Allesandria, a big junction which we reached about 8.45 p.m. we availed ourselves of the big buffet there, and I and some of the lads in my party fared very sumptuously off bread, cheese and wine. Tres bon! Most of us were feeling tired, for owing to the heat and dust, the journey this day had been fatiguing, but after a halt and feed, we managed to summon up sufficient vim to cheer lustily in response to the only half hearted compliment made by a big crowd of onlookers.

At Voghera in Lombardy we saw one of the big factories of the Fiat Motor Company, and many of the girls exchanged souvenirs with our lads. We halted here for an hour and a half, and had tea (10.45 p.m.). As in France, so in Italy, these rest halts were manned by British soldiers, and I should imagine that at some places at least, the life of these men was anything but attractive, far removed as they were from any centre where there was amusement or recreation, the only diversion the passing of troop trains, their existence was monotonous in the extreme.

---

108 Mobile Italian light infantry wearing distinctive wide brimmed hats, decorated with black feathers.

August 25th

The well known town of Parma and the big town of Reggio were packed during early morning. The district hereabouts was more interesting, the vineyards stretching farflung on either side. The vines, a big variety, were trained over the lower branches of trees, and luscious fruit hung in big bunches sometimes temptingly near the train. Had the train halted anywhere near, the vineyards would have been raided. Here too, the people appeared more industrially inclined, and pretty barefooted women and girls were often seen passing along the roads. We crossed several rivers during the day, tributaries of the River Po and to the westward the peaks of the Maritime Alps could be seen. An interesting sight was the ploughing with teams of bullocks, as many as ten being yoked to a plough. The interest of many of the places we passed through was due to our having read about them in novels or histories. Modena was one of these, and I remembered its connection with Catherine de Medici. We passed this town about breakfast time. Regarding the houses, those in the country districts were ugly. The walls were invariably plastered, and originally lividly coloured, but under the ravages of weather, colours had faded. The favourite colour scheme appeared to be wide stripes of light blue, white, and light brown. But in the towns, many splendidly built houses and public buildings delighted the eye. This applies specially to Bologna which we reached about 9 a.m. On the western side of the line, a magnificent church, possibly an art treasure, stood on a high hill around which and running up the sides was a high wall which in itself was an architectural beauty. The dire need of rain was most apparent in this district, the ground being seen parched and cracked.

Here I must testify to the grace of God found sufficient for every need. As a general rule, I always require quiet, and to some extent, comfort, to enjoy my Bible, but in spite of heat, dust, and sundry distraction, I enjoyed and profited by reading my Testament. Today, the grace received was so pronounced that I made a special note of it in my journal from which of course I am getting my material for this record. It will be seen later that I proved this sterling promise of God under the queerest and most unfavourable circumstances.

At 10.30 a.m. we pulled into Faenza, the first rest camp in Italy. After disembarking, we marched to the camp ¾ mile away, situated on a big, more or less barren plain. It was a huge camp, and we found thousands of troops there including a big draft of seamen and H.M.A.S.[109] men bound for Macedonia. We arrived at rather an unlucky time, for owing to a rupture in one of the mains, the water supply had been practically cut off. It was desperately hot, and so of course we were looking forward to a good wash. We were informed that no water would be available until 5 p.m. But even then, we were allowed only a water bottle full each so we shared up, and six of us washed in about two quarts of water. With reference to the shortage and times of washing water, we had a saying when inquiring how many had previously washed in some water, "How many deep is it?" I have a note of an occasion when a bucket of water became twenty two deep before the remains were finally thrown away, that is, twenty two had washed in it. I was the eleventh, and then the water was – well – pretty solid. But it was a wash any how. Football matches were the order of the day, and fierce conflicts were waged in the fierce heat to the no small interest of crowds of natives who must have thought the men mad.

Aug 26th

The next day being Sunday, we were early acquainted of the fact by the discordant tolling of numerous church bells. One was reminded of blasphemous hours spent in bed on Sunday mornings at home when our early Sabbath slumbers were rudely disturbed by the tolling of bells near by. My ablutions this morning were performed with the aid of a mug of water and the corner of my towel. Later on, we were paraded with other troops and marched to the town and had a good swill in

109 His Majesty's Australian Ship.

an open drain. I don't think anyone troubled to question either the origin or course of the water supply. What with Sunday parades etc. it was hard to realise it was Sunday, and I felt out of tune all day, but a good read of my Sword helped me to sense the Presence. When we paraded for departure at 6.30 p.m., a big Sunday crowd of onlookers gave tone to the proceedings. The women folk, all of whom wore mantillas,[110] looked quite gay, and the colours of dress, of men and women made a very pretty scene. After entraining again, we left F. about 8.50 p..m. There was a fairly enthusiastic crowd to see us off, but one missed the enthusiasm of France.

At Forli, we received orders to put all lights out as we were nearing the coast and getting within the zone raided by air and sea. My bed was an uncomfortable one, but I had now got used to sleeping anywhere and on anything, and slept soundly. We had now been a week on our journey East. Before dropping asleep, by some chance my thoughts were York wards, and I calculated Millie would be at chapel. Then I thought of courting days, and smiled and sighed over sundry reminiscences. Memory, what a wonderful thing! At once, blessed and cursed, a source of joy and a reservoir of pain. But under grace, invariably a God given faculty, and this evening, I fell asleep with a heart bubbling with gratitude to God for what made the memories so sweet, encouraging and strengthening.

Aug 27th

The following day we were passing through the Abbruzzo Province, and a pretty sight met our gaze when we awoke. We were travelling dead south, the shimmering sea lay on our east, and far across the plain, mountains to the west. We noticed that the natives here were darker skinned and more sturdily built than further north.

A treat awaited us a Castleamara where we arrived about 8.30. We disentrained, and were marched through the town to

---

110 Traditional lace veils or shawls.

the beach, where bathing drawers were issued and we gambolled like great kiddies in the sea. Oh it was fine. Needless to say, in spite of the discipline, it required a lot of shouting by the NCOs in charge before they got us all out again. Then to add to the pleasure of the event, fruit was on sale at controlled, and therefore cheap prices. Splendid black or white grapes at 1d per large bunch; large peaches @ 3 for 2d; tomatoes 3 for 1d, Victoria plums 3 for 1d; etc. I personally gorged with grapes. After bathing, we had breakfast but I confess I could eat but little after the fruit banquet. We didn't leave C. until 12.15. From my map, I was able to "make out" some of the mountains to the west. Passing along some of us remarked the peculiar hand waving of the natives who greeted us. I imagine there is something of meaning in these "hand waves." The French waved their hands from the wrist outwards suggestive of "Bon voyage," whereas the Italians waved their hands fingers inwards, suggestive of a safe and quick return.

The Blue Adriatic alongside which we ran for several miles, and the snow capped mountains far to the westward, was a somewhat refreshing if tantalising effect as we sweated from the intense heat. With reference to the sea, the complete absence of any kind of craft was very noticeable. At every halt, we seized the short opportunity to wash under stand pipes and taps, and caused no doubt, more than passing interest to the natives as sometimes stripped to the waist, we splashed and spluttered. But in spite of these intervals, the troops as a whole looked blackguardly dirty, the strong wind blowing clouds of dust into the carriages. During the afternoon, we passed a train load of leave men from Salonika on their way to Blighty, most of them riding in trucks. A wonderfully pretty lagoon[111] was passed about 4 p.m., the background of the Gargano Mts being reflected in the sapphire coloured water. Foggia, a big town was reached about 6.50 p.m. and here we halted for tea and a wash. The officers took advantage of the long halt to go out and have a look around the town and this revived the complaint bitterly made by many of the men. At no place were we allowed to leave either camp or station precincts, and at the larger stations, the

---

111 Lago Di Lesina probably.

buffets were usually "out of bounds". It must be remembered that many of the men were socially the superiors of the officers, some of whom were of that class of snobs which is the curse of the commissioned ranks in the new army, and who were exceedingly conscious of their unusual rank superiority. I shall have more to record about officers later on in this record. As regards the extra privileges complained of above, granted that there was the danger of some of the men creating trouble, it should be remarked that the officers were no exemplars, for one at least was distinguished by his constant drunken state, and corresponding bestial conduct.

Just before we entered Foggia, an Italian aeroplane manoeuvred overhead, and appeared to be acting as a patrol. A feature of our halt here was the gangs of Italians moving from carriage to carriage offering change in local currency for English souvenirs and treasury notes. Of course, many were too green to see through this little sharp practice and were satisfied with the face value 9½d per lira whereas the then exchange value was only 7½d, or to put it in exchange terms, these financiers were giving about 25.26 lira for £1, the then market value being 32 liras. I noticed that in 1918 it rose to 46.30 liras.

We left F about 9 p.m. as, as an instance of strange "Bethels"[112], I record that I sat on the footboard in the rear of the car and had a very fine and helpful time with God. The rattle of the car drowned my somewhat subdued singing.

August 28th

The following morning, about 6.15 we stopped at Ostuni, a very pretty and picturesque city on a hill surrounded by cedars and olive trees. I though of Zion[113] and wondered if I ever should see the Holy City. Brindisi was reached at 7.30 when we ran alongside a dock siding and so had a good view of the several

---

112 A place where Jacob had a special encounter with God and called it Beth-el: the house of God, saying "God was surely in this place and I did not know it." Genesis 28:16-18.

113 Jerusalem.

ships in the harbour. There were signs of visits by Austrian air raiders who I understand made frequent sorties to this port and Taranto. Brindisi did not appear very attractive, the houses appearing covered with the white dust which blew around in clouds. A "sea-pig" (naval airship) cruising around interested us. Here I had a welcome shave and clean up, and purchased a couple of singlets and so cast an exceedingly mucky shirt. We left B at 10 a.m. And soon afterwards passed Mesagne which was very interesting on account of its presenting an unusually oriental appearance. The buildings near the railway were beautified with grand palms and oleanders, in fact the scene reminded me forcibly of India. Hereabouts it was a great fig growing country, and the natives showered luscious green figs on us as we slowly passed along. In various places, we saw great squares of picked figs drying in the sun. The youngsters that lined the track asked for what at first we couldn't interpret, but soon found out to be "bullee bif" (bully beef). Scores of tins were soon exchanged for figs and grapes. Coming into sight of the Mar Piccolo (Little Sea) a splendid natural harbourage at the sea end of which stands Taranto, we saw several ships of different nationalities riding at anchor, the most interesting of which were a Japanese cruiser and a French battleship. At a point at the head of the harbour, we reversed engines, and after a short journey performed in a long and trying time, reached the end of our long rail journey at 3.30 p.m., after a days travel, at Cimino, the next camp 2 ½ miles from Taranto. Our first sight and experience of the place was anything but inspiring. The heat was tropical, and the camp was almost barren and ankle deep in fine white dust which blew in all directions. After a deal of fuss and sulphurous language, we disentrained and were arched to the corner of the huge camp allotted to our troop train. I and 63 others were herded (that's the word) in a marquee without floor boards or blankets. We met some men going on leave from Egypt, and they said that this was really worse than anything experienced there, an exaggeration, as we afterwards found out, but really not so very far from the truth. Another disappointment awaited us, for when we found the canteen, expecting to be able to get a feed, we found it minus biscuits or anything cheap enough to make a feed of. At dusk, we prepared to settle for the night. That meant sleeping in the thick dust, so my chum and I decided to "sleep out" and so putting on our overcoats, and using our kit bags for pillows, stretched ourselves on a firm bit of ground outside the marquee and were soon sound asleep. We all registered a devout hope that our stay at Cimino would be a short one. Very fortunately, nobody had the remotest expectation of staying as long as we did, viz. five weeks.

Departing from the "diary" style, I'll record the interesting events of those five weeks.

Cimino

The camp was just a huge canvas town, which had, when we arrived, been erected to accommodate the thousands of troops passing to and from Macedonia and Egypt. Before we left, the majority of these tents had been replaced by Mission Huts, and stone buildings erected for the various headquarters officers, messes etc. I learned from those in the know, that it was intended for use during and after the war, and eventually would be taken over by the Italian Government. The single line railway was soon after our arrival duplicated, the Cimino sidings becoming long and numerous. Another structural feature was the wharf which was built in an amazingly short time with the aid of hordes of the Egyptian Labour Corps. Ships ran alongside, and their cargoes stored in huge warehouses in less than a month from the time when the site was a barren bit of foreshore. The position of the Mar Piccolo may be understood when the shape of South Italy is remembered as like a foot. The Gulf of Taranto forms the hollow ball of the foot, and the Mar Piccolo is really a big lagoon at the top right hand corner of the Gulf as it curves downwards towards the "heel". Taranto is at the entrance to the lagoon which is almost land locked, the entrance being only just sufficiently wide enough to permit the passage of a first class man-o-war.

Here I ought to explain that our stay of five weeks was quite unforeseen and was due to the breakdown of the boat that should have taken us to Alexandria eight days after our arrival. On at least five occasions we had notice to be ready to shift, only to be badly disappointed each time, so much so that we eventually took no notice of the "warnings", and it became a catch phrase "We're sailing tomorrow."

The day following our arrival, I was made responsible for the letters, and had to collect them and assist in censoring the same. It was as may be imagined an interesting job. Our officer who was a real gentleman and who took the greatest interest in the troops, an exceptional officer accordingly, gave every encouragement to the lads to write, even going to the extent when no writing material could be had from the canteen, to send to Taranto for supplies, selling the same at a loss to himself. He was most considerate too as a censor, only erasing what was positively verboten; and if necessary returning the letter to the delinquent for revision. In contrast to other officers, he rarely commented on what he read, and even then only in the case of humorous items when for instance, a snake killed in the camp ranged in length according to the various versions from 12 inches to four feet. I nearly fell down and worshipped him when he severely castigated one young snob who ridiculed the love passages written by a man to his wife. The letters revealed one splendid trait common to the lads and that was they never complained to their folk about their discomfort, but were always cheerful. With regard to censoring, I in common with all others, no matter how much confidence I trust we had in the various censors, could never lose the feeling of restraint when writing, and they, who, as foolish as myself are head over heels in love, could never bring themselves to express those ebbulitions[114] that well up in one's heart as they write to the loved ones. Imagine yourselves, you who are in love, in a similar circumstance, and you will appreciate that we always felt this to be a real hardship. Green envelopes,[115] which

---

114 Ebullition – a sudden outburst or display.
115 Specially printed envelopes which could be sealed and were not subject to censorship, provided the correspondent promised "on honour" not to include any

we didn't get until we got to Egypt were therefore thrice blessed and welcome to sender and recipient alike.

Cimino had one big advantage and that was the unlimited supply of water and sea bathing. The dust which invariably blew about the camp, produced ludicrous results with the men who used to wander around looking like millers, therefore the facilities for washing and bathing were thoroughly appreciated. The bathing hours were restricted on account of the intense heat to mornings and late afternoon, when the beach used to be alive with naked soldiery.

Our big grievance was the Canteen. The charges were exorbitant, and usually prohibitive as regards certain luxuries. Now the present system of canteens was supposedly devised in the interests of the troops, but with my knowledge of what canteens were like previous to the inauguration of the system, I have no hesitation in saying that the Navy and Army Canteen Board is a scandal and the troops robbed right and left. There were occasions later when we found them a boon and when articles could be bought at reasonable prices judged by home market standards, but I never know at any time of goods that were not sold greatly above their real value, for be it remembered there were no transport charges of any kind levied on the goods sold, and no salaries supposed to be paid to officials. All goods such as tobacco on which duty is usually paid, were supplied duty free, and yet as an instance, cigarettes of only a fair quality were sold at Cimino at 3/2 for 50. Again, for some reason this canteen was invariably short of the most desired articles such as biscuits, cigarettes and tobacco, chocolate, writing materials, candles etc. Beer however, was usually plentiful. No need for comments. The size of the camp demanded better supplies which easily could and should have been forthcoming.

At first, there were no facilities for religious services, but owing to the untiring efforts and steady persistence of a Wesleyan padre, one of the only two padres in the whole camp,

---

military information. Their use was especially sought by married men.

the other being an R.C.,[116] a reading marquee was eventually erected, and a concert platform built near by, so that we enjoyed some really fine services. Mr Kelley the Wes padre was an A.1. man, and no amount of praise is undeserved. But personally, I best enjoyed those quiet times I had "on my own" behind timber stacks, under trees, by the sea, or beside a bush. Oh how sweet those times were. Every spot a Beracah,[117] every place a Bethel. Only those who have had to seek for such blessings can realise what I felt, only those who have ever been denied the usual means of grace, the quiet room, the hushed stillness, the help of books etc. can sympathise with my difficulties. And yet, rarely in ordinary life have I enjoyed such an overwhelming sense of the Master's nearness. He revealed Himself so fully, that I got into the habit of conversational talks with Him. In this connection, I enjoyed the occasional contact with other Christians. Especially was this so when a siege artillery draft passing through included about half a dozen lads who had formed a branch of the Soldier's Christian Association.[118] We held one meeting under some trees, and a glorious time it was.

It will be readily guessed that time hung heavily on our hands, especially during the day time. Some fine concerts were occasionally held. But our officer here again proved his interestedness by sundry efforts to keep the boys amused. He devised a shell collecting competition, water sports, route marches with halts for an interesting talk on some aspect of the natural environs, debates, discussions, sing songs, whist drives etc. The bulk of the organisation of these fell upon me as his "lieutenant," but I always enjoyed the sometimes hard work. The debates were strangely enough perhaps the biggest success. We discovered plenty of "talking talent" amongst our gunners,

---

116 Roman Catholic.

117 Beracah: Hebrew for Blessing, a valley named at the time of King Jehoshaphat in 2 Chronicles 20:26.

118 In 1887 The Soldiers' Christian Association was formed, becoming The Soldiers' and Airmen's Christian Association when the Royal Air Force was formed. In 1938 the Army Scripture Readers and SACA amalgamated and in 1952 the name, The Soldiers' and Airmen's Scripture Readers Association was adopted. Usually known by the acronym, SASRA.

and the fame of our efforts got so abroad, that some of the officers and nurses passing through asked to be allowed to attend. A rather funny incident happened one evening when the subject was the old old one of "Should Bachelors be taxed." A fussy, self-important, somewhat "soft" Captain who had recently taken over temporarily the duties of Camp Adjutant, the usual official being sick, was told as a joke by some young bloods that a political meeting was being held in our section, so he pompously strode into the marquee and ordered the cessation of hostilities. Explanations were forthcoming from the chairman, and the disconcerted "fuss pot" retired looking very red and foolish.

Personally, I usually found plenty to interest me. I was specially interested in the study of the different types of men met. I will only mention one impression. That was the reversion to type of so many individuals. Men who clearly filled decent social positions in civil life, unconsciously shed their veneers and at least as regards language degenerated to the level of the worst. Restraint was abandoned and when beer was plentiful, they successfully emulated the foulest of the "boozers". Their general conduct was worthy of the slums, and their appearance oft-times like tramps. Granted that it required a strong individuality and strength of will to maintain a high level of character and conduct, there was no excuse for these men, and their declension was a striking instance of the sham and veneer so characteristic of our boasted civilisation.

The varying dialects of speech heard in the camp was also interesting. One could hear the soft burr of the west countryman, the guttural grind of the Glasgow Scotchman, the sharp, staccato ear slapping accent of the cockney, the wide mouthed almost snarl of the north countryman, the even timed and clean pronounciation [sic] of the Welsh, the rippling, rolling, rattle of the Irishman. I early on was able to almost infallibly "place" a man by his speech.

Taranto was out of bounds to the troops unless in possession of a pass which were only infrequently granted, and then only for special reason. So I was delighted when my officer offered me a pass one day to go with the caterer for the Officers Mess to purchase goods for same. Taranto is famous by reason of its being the birthplace of Esculapius, the "Father of Medicine", and was known as a sea port in 500BC. The day I visited it was holiday and so most of the people were in holiday garb and the cafés doing a roaring trade. We visited some of these cafés and found some enterprising enough to cater for English tastes in the matter of whisky, beer, rum etc. Personally, I favoured a refreshing iced fruit drink. The streets were fine large clean thoroughfares, and the buildings for the main part artistic and imposing. The ancient part of the town stands separate from the modern part, and ruins of the old city can still be seen. I saw two interesting sights, a funeral, with the gaily coloured hearse, the score or more of professional girl mourners garbed in a sort of grey red gowns, the nuns and the friars. The other was the coming ashore of hundreds of Italian sailors, looking splendidly smart in their white clothes. Outside the churches were boards and crucifixes with the various implements of the Passion attached thereto, e.g. a hammer, a spear, nails, rope, ladder etc. Of course, as a shell backed[119] Protestant I felt rather disgusted at these very crude "aids". From one point on the harbour wall I got a fine view of the harbour, a splendid anchorage. Some British boats including the "Lord Nelson" were there. As stated previously, the only entrance to the harbour and inland sea beyond is through a narrow channel wide enough to just allow the passage of a battleship. Over this channel and connecting the ancient and modern parts of the town is a swing bridge, a fine engineering feat. I was fully occupied in seeing the sights the whole time I was in the town, and I was quite sorry when I had to return to the camp. After the monotony of Cimino the trip was a real tonic and did me good.

During the last week of our stay, we shifted from tents into newly erected Mission huts, just in time to escape some heavy rains.

---

119 Idiom usually used to describe a sailor who had crossed the equator or a veteran sailor. The latter probably intended here: "a veteran Protestant."

Yes, the days hung very heavily in spite of all attempts to arrange amusement, and often I lost count of the days. I got into the habit of distinguishing days by blessings, but as I am somewhat of a spiritual weathercock subject to occasional "down" days, even this method of reckoning the passage of the days didn't quite prove satisfactory. So we were all hugely delighted when after frequent "alarms" we got definite orders and packed up, and boarded the "Snaefell" on Oct 3rd.

[Oct 3rd]

The "Snaefell" in the piping days of peace was an I. Of Man steamer plying between Douglas and Liverpool.[120] As we saw it, it was fitted up as a troopship with false side and temporary messes. We had a distinguished passenger in Admiral Kuroski, a Russian, who was travelling to Alexandria. The arrangements on board were surprisingly good for such a small boat, but of course, we were closely packed. Immediately we embarked, we were issued with life belts, a hammock and a blanket, and then, before we could get settled, had to turn out for boat drill. We were told off to our various boats, the tackle explained to us, and orders given as to procedure in the event of a collision with a tin fish[121] or an iron ration.[122] My station was at a collapsible raft which somehow I didn't fancy so serviceable as a boat. However, I had no qualms of fear for by sea or by land "He knoweth the way I take"[123] and I even dwell under the shadow of the Almighty.[124]

We felt like cheering when soon after 4 p.m. the engines started and we began to progress down the Mar Piccolo towards Taranto. We were however in for a slight disappointment, for we had almost got to the harbour, when we stopped, then

---

120 Later sunk June 1918 after a torpedo attack west of Malta.
121 Torpedo.
122 Shell or ammunition or some kind.
123 Based on Job 23:10, a number of popular American hymns made this the refrain, including *Through the wearisome hours of a sorrowful night*, S.M. Walsh, 1881 and *The clouds may hover o'er me*, A.A. Payn, 1907.
124 Psalm 91:1.

turned back and moored up again to our previous anchorage. Submarines were reported outside the harbour so we turned back. We were only a little disappointed, for we felt that as long as we remained on board, we were on our way at last to Egypt. So we rigged up our hammocks, and prepared for slumber. There was some fun and – bad language over the cramped accommodation, for the hammocks were slung so close together, that we bumped into each other, and in some cases tipped another man out. My head was well fenced in on one side by the feet of a man who I'll declare wore size 14 in boots. Whether or not the combination of aromas from feet; mouths; deck and hold was inductive to sleep, I slept well in spite of bumps from passengers walking underneath during the night.

[Oct 4th]

Early the following morning, we joined in the process of swabbing decks, after which we were left to our own designs. During the afternoon, the troops were allowed to go overboard for a swim, and in spite of the fact that I am only an indifferent swimmer, I couldn't resist the temptation of a 20ft dive. It was fine. Some of the lads were experts and gave a fine display of fancy diving from the forecastle deck, a height of about 40ft.

We set sail again about 5.30 p.m., and this time proceeded without a stop seawards. All the men-o-war flew their Russian flag in honour of our distinguished super-cargo, an Italian dreadnought manning ship, a pretty sight. A remarkable sight was a half sunken Italian dreadnought, keel upmost, lying surrounded by salvage tugs. This was the result of a mysterious explosion several weeks before. A big French troopship laden with French troops from Salonika got moving behind us, and escorted by three destroyers, we passed through the exit to the harbour, past an island fort to a point of which a sausage balloon[125] was moored, and so out into the open sea. After awhile just before dark, the French troopers and two destroyers

---

125 A kite balloon used for observation.

separated from us leaving us to the care of H.M.T.B.D.[126] "Pincher." This naval sleuthound then commenced the procedure carried out the whole journey to Alexandria, of crossing and recrossing our bow and occasionally our stern while our boat pursued a zig zag course moving always in an opposite direction to the escort. One got the impression of a terrier running ahead of a retriever, leading the way to some desired goal. When it got dark, the phosphorescent wake and waves were prettily interesting.

[Oct 5th]

On the following morning Oct 5th we sighted Corfu about 9 a.m., the Kaiser's Meditterranean [sic] retreat, now a Serbian rest camp. We were having a beautiful passage, the sea being wonderfully blue. The last occasion I sailed on the Meditterranean, we were confined below closed hatches for three days on account of the rough seas.[127] The crew had the usual pets on board, a very tame Maltese cockerel, a dove, and a pup. The cocky was the favourite. We zigzagged frequently hereabouts probably on account of our passing so many small islands which would afford fine bases for the unterseeboots.[128] The day was uneventful but at night under a glorious canopy of stars, I had a talk with the Friend. I have all the usual susceptibility to the influence of church and chapel, but I ever felt God nearer when worshipping beneath the Creator's heavenly vault. The fo'c'sle[129] this evening was a Bethel indeed.

[Oct 6th]

We sighted Crete next morning about 7.30, and after a pleasant run around the coast, entered Suda Bay about 9 a.m. The entrance to the harbour is very pretty, surrounded as it is

---

126 His Majesty's Torpedo Boat Destroyer. Pincher was a Beagle class destroyer.
127 Travel from India? Or Mesopotamia?
128 U-boat (Submarine).
129 Forecastle – the foredeck of the ship.

by high cliffs and mountains. The water too was astonishingly clear, and various form of marine life could be clearly seen, especially the monster jelly fish. The entrance to the harbour proper used to be guarded by two island rock forts, but these are now dismantled and apparently uninhabited. Just inside these "gates", lay the wreck of the mined transport "Minnewaska", a big ship which carried several thousand troops when struck all of whom were however saved. Several English drifters lay at anchor, one of which I had seen at Hull in the halcyon day of peace. The harbour was well packed with all sorts of craft including several coaling vessels alongside one of which we eventually moored. I remembered a previous coaling experience years ago at Port Said, so I was glad when about noon, all the troops were taken off in lighters[130] to the shore near the ubiquitous Y.M.C.A.[131] Here I lunched off pineapples, biscuits and ginger beer and listened awhile to a good pianist, one of the lads from the boat playing Rachmaninoffs Prelude, Chansons Trist, a Beethoven's Nocturne, Brahms No5 Hungarian Dance etc. etc. Oh! It was fine. But the inconsiderable fathead played "The Perfect Day" and of course I had a discomforting vision of dear old Haxby where I think I had last heard it. A swim in the crystal sea was not one of the least pleasures. The time passed swiftly and it was soon 5 p.m. when we returned to our ship. About 6.15 we were off again and running along the north side of the island got out into the open sea again. Chatting to some of the crew, I found that one of the stokers was the son of a councillor of a Midland town. He had cleared out of home without consent or knowledge of his people, and joined the Navy, and was unfortunate enough to get his present berth.

A strong breeze sprang up during the night, and the following morning found the visages of some of the lads less cheerful than previously, for the boat pitched and rolled rather nastily. Seasickness was fairly common, but I again was one of the unsympathetic scoffers. There was no padre aboard, so although Sunday, we had no service. Another war time change,

---

130 A flat-bottomed transport barge.
131 Young Men's Christian Association.

for in the service it used to be the rule for the captain, in the absence of a parson to read the lesson on Sundays. However, I had a good course of "Sword exercise" and felt the presence of the Holy Spirit. I thought of our sabbaths at home, and felt very grateful that the recollection of those pearls of days was so sweet and full of remembered blessings. Thank God, my weekends of the past few years are worth recalling. Naturally I felt very wistful about 6 p.m. And longed to slide into the pew at Groves or Haxby. Ah well, I could still help in those services, and I believe I did. Prayer has a wonderful reach and influence.

Full of expectation, we were early astir on Monday, the 8th, and at 6 a.m. could make out the tops of towers, factory chimneys etc. of Alexandria. We appeared to run along the coast for a distance before passing the breakwater, and it was not before 10 a.m. when we finally bumped the quay side. Egypt at last. The wharves, quays and dock sides were abounding in troops, and one felt somehow at a part of Blighty. The intense heat however spoiled the effect. I had my first sight of the caterpillar tractors here, queer contraptions, very noisy and as regards speed, like some folk, all blow and no go. After sundry and many preliminaries, we disembarked about 1.30 p.m. And set foot on the mystic Land of the Pharaohs. Ebenezer.[132]

Part II On the Desert

About 2 p.m. we formed up and marched out of the docks, and through the typically Eastern streets. You may be sure we were all agape as we marched and the queer houses, shops, sherbet sellers, veiled women, Arabs, fellaheen[133] were all objects of the greatest interest and often of caustic mirth. That

---

132 1 Samuel 7:12 "Ebenezer - Thus far the Lord has helped us" reference to the name given to a stone placed by Samuel as a reminder of God's help.
133 Arabic peasant or agricultural labourer.

peculiar, indefinable "sweetish" smell, so characteristic of the Indian bazaar was here very pronounced. I think it is due to the aromatic sweets and foods, and the oil with which so many natives anoint themselves. Sundry "Gyppo" boys ran alongside us offering various articles for sale. At one point, we got into the electric cars, and rode on these for about 2 miles to Mustapha Camp where we were to be accommodated. As I never had the opportunity to visit Alexandria, my impressions are rather vague and confined to results of this journey. On the eastern outskirts of the city, the buildings are exceedingly fine, and suggest civic wealth and prosperity. The public buildings, especially the "Bourse,"[134] Post Office, Anglo-Egyptian Exchange, are built on a lavish scale. By the way the official language here is French. Near Mustapha is a splendidly laid out race course which is, I gathered, heavily patronised by the Alexandrians. I am writing all this while awaiting removal "down the line" for embarkation home, and I hope to have a chance to inspect "Alick" before I sail. If I do, the result will be given later. But I opine, even from my very casual observations, that it deserves all the praise bestowed upon it for its magnificence. A feature of the streets was the splendid equestrian turnouts, the blood Arab horses being specially beautiful. After all, a good show of horses and carriage have a finer effect than the most gorgeous motor car. The cosmopolitan crowd of soldiers and civilians was also very interesting.

The camp at Mustapha Pasha has no extraordinary interest, just a huge canvas town. Of course, our arrival there was immediately followed by our enquiry regarding letters, and after our long deprivation of news from home, there was huge delight when I eventually got hold of several bags of letters and proceeded to sort them out. My share was very welcome as you may guess. Therefore it was rather a late hour when I sallied forth on the search for supper, and found my way into a home[135] owned and conducted by a Miss Carney, a fine type of Christian

134 An exchange.
135 Soldiers' Home.

lady. A meeting was in progress when I got there, and needless to record, I promptly joined in.

The day after our arrival[136] was mainly spent in inspections and parades, and general refitting for the work we came out to do. I and some of the other N.C.Os from Winchester had a big disappointment, for owing to our delay at Taranto, the posts we were sent out to fill had been given to others, so we dropped our stripes, reverted to gunners and were posted to different batteries. I found I was posted to 181st Heavy Battery R.G.A.,[137] a battery preparing to enter the firing line. However, the edge was taken off my disappointment, for I felt that somehow or other, God was overruling for my good. We were not due to leave "Alick" for five or six days, so we set to work to pass the time as profitably as possible. When possible, I went for walks around and saw something of the rural life of the natives. Irrigation canals abounded, and very fine field and garden produce grew everywhere. We found also that the plague of flies has only been partially suspended.[138] They were everywhere, and on everything. Bathing of course was a favourite pastime, especially as the sandy shore offered such good walking. Most of my evenings were spent at Lord Kitchener's Soldiers Home, a part of the work of the Mission to Mediterranean Garrisons. The ladies there were exceptionally fine, and rendered incalculable service for God and the soldiers. I must mention here that I owe it to Miss Mitchell, one of the said ladies, for our inspiration to service as a soldier that proved during the whole of my active service in Egypt and Palestine, an uplift and an encouragement. She spoke at an evening meeting on "Prophecy" and gave an interpretation of those prophecies relating to the restoration of Israel, showing clearly that the present war out here was accomplishing the fulfilment of these. She told her huge audience that they were in the truest sense of the word, crusaders, instruments of God for the working out of His wonderful purposes. She told of the doubtful character of the old crusaders, and pleaded that the

136 Now 9th October.
137 Royal Garrison Artillery.
138 Humorous reference to the plagues of Egypt at the time of Moses.

new crusaders as God's chosen men give their lives to Him, to live for Him, and if it be His will, to die for Him. The interest of the hearers was intense, and few if any left the hall without a new ideal, and a strengthened purpose. Contrast this address with some we know of as delivered by certain padres. From that day to this, I have never lost the sense of God's possession, and "fed up" as I have been often, I have ever remembered my high calling. Furthermore, the message came just at the hour of need, for I was still sore from disappointment, and lacked the interest in my erstwhile profession without which military life would be a day long painful servitude.

Of course, the Home had a bar, and sold suppers at cheap rates. We were very puzzled over the currency at first, for most of our money was English, and piastre[139] standard of 2½d was confusing. Eventually, we got used to it, but one peculiar result was that in thinking in terms of piastres, our valuation was in terms of pence, that is, that we unconsciously judged the price of say a 3d article as 3 piastres, and spent our money accordingly. This illusion was fostered by the high price of nearly everything, and for instance we bought apples at 3 for 1pt. and felt just as we should have felt if the price had been 3 for 1d. In short, we spent piastres as we should pence.

The cries of the hawkers were a never ending source of hilarity, especially the news vendors. Here are some of their cries, " 'Gyptian Mail, plenty good news, British transport sunk"; " 'Gyptian Mail, very good paper, very nice, very sweet, very clean"; "Plenty sweet 'Gyptian Mail, very nice paper".

Before passing from events at Mustapha, I feel I must mention the awful, indescribably awful vice prevalent in Alex.[140] The description of it couldn't be related verbally, let alone written, sufficient to record that no estimate by anyone ignorant of the conditions obtaining in Cairo and Alex of the possible veriest depths of human depravity could approach the actual facts. Of course, my knowledge is only from hearsay, but

---

139 Unit of currency in French-speaking colonies.
140 Prostitution was well known in Cairo and Alexandria, and other soldiers' writings
    describe surprise or sadness at its prevalence.

much as I know of what occurs in Rangoon, Madras, Bombay and some French towns, nothing ever approximates to what can be seen nightly in these cities of Egypt.[141] And here's the damning fact, it all goes on with the full knowledge of the civil and military authorities, yes, and in certain cases, with their tacit sanction. The wickedness, which goes far beyond anything suggested in Scripture, is witnessed by, and up to certain degrees indulged in by mere lads sometimes, who had positively no conception of such evil before they came out here. My battery is of an average strength of about 200, and out of that number, I assert not less than 75 have either witnessed, or taken part, or both, in this vice; and some of these, mere lads below the age of 25, two at least being below 20 years of age. Many of these men are by birth, education, speech and bearing, clearly from good families, and I care not what they may become on re-entrance to civic life, they are, and will ever be moral lepers in a greater or lesser degree according to strength of character. Furthermore, one cannot escape hearing the details of their experiences, and even although as in my case one doesn't allow the thoughts to dwell on the subject, he is affected, he cannot help being so, for the simple knowledge of such things contaminates. I never felt so doubtful of God's oversight as in this matter, for I should imagine that Sodom and Gomorrah were Gardens of Eden to Alexandria and Cairo. My difficulty here is to pass on to the next subject, for as a Christian, and a Britisher, I feel a personal grievance in this matter, and I too am one of the sufferers.

We were all made fearful guys the other day before we left the camp, when we were given close cropped hair cuts. Later on I shaved my moustache off and looked about as prepossessing as a Walmgate Bar tout.[142] I'd dearly have liked to have run across

---

141 Woodward notes similar experiences and feelings from other soldiers in David Woodward, *Forgotten Soldiers of the First World War* (Stroud: Tempus, 2007), pp43-48.

142 Walmgate Bar is one of the gates in York city wall. It was a notorious slum area in the 19th Century, attracting hawkers and traders. Previously, it was renowned for the heads which were displayed on the bar in the seventeenth century, including that of Robert Hillyard, who called himself Robin of Holderness, who was executed after leading a tax rebellion in 1469. Bryant's comparison to the touts might also be an echo of the skull-like features he'd taken on since the hair-cut!

my missus, and I wondered what she would say. I could guess one or two terms she would use.

On the evening of Oct 15th we marched to the station en route to the desert. The Master gave me Psalm 121 as a tonic. My chum, who had kept his stripe, one he got in France and therefore sacrosanct, was in charge of a ration party, and he got me with him in a van. The others were packed very uncomfortably tight in 3rd Class carriages containing wooden seats; so I felt fortunate. I think we nearly all felt sorry that the journey was undertaken at night, for we would have preferred travelling by day so as to see the country as we passed through it. We arrived early at El Kantara, our destination early the following morning. We found here a huge camp which had sprung up in what previously was barren desert. Kantara is on the Canal railway which for its great length skirts the Suez Canal to the south. It has an ancient history, but there is very little remaining of its buildings. Of the greatest interest to me were the bridges, built on wooden piles which had been built after the attempted Turkish invasion of Egypt. Fairly severe fighting took place here, but the attempted crossing was further south. Kantara afforded my first view of the unsurpassingly wonderful changes effected by the military. Roads had been built around and across hitherto trackless desert along which we saw long strings of camels, laden with war paraphernalia wending their slow way towards the far off firing line. Wonder of wonders, L&S.W.R.[143] railway engines dragged long lines of trucks, some of which had also come from England. Hard on the heels of the advancing troops, a main road had been built for foot traffic and light motors, by laying across the sand stretches of wire netting of the poultry run type. It needs but little imagination to understand what this meant to the men of Shank's cavalry[144]. The track for heavier traffic such as lorries

---

143 London and South Western Railway.

144 This term means "on foot." It refers originally to the shin bones or lower leg being the means of transport. Also known as "Shanks's pony" in Britain or "Shanks's Mare" in the USA. Apparently it was capitalised as it was thought (wrongly) to originate from a person called Shanks, whose company produced a horse-drawn lawnmower that required the worker to walk behind in order to guide it. It appears Shank's Cavalry is Philip's own version of the phrase.

and guns ran parallel to this, and one marvelled at the feat of endurance amongst the draught animals in dragging for scores of miles, heavily laden vehicles across the loose sand. One and one only well worn track could be distinguished, and that was the oldest highway in the world along which the travellers long before the time of Abraham and Abraham himself passed. In fact, all the scripturally recorded journeys from Palestine to Egypt took place along this road. Six weeks previous to my visit, there were but few tents, and only this and the wire road extant. Now there were YMCAs, Church Army and Salvation Army marquees, and all the usual perquisites of a huge encampment, about 10sq miles in dimension.

I lost my chum here, who left during the evening for his battery. I felt lonely.

We were at Kantara until late the following evening. Previous to re-entraining, I had a chance to get to a YMCA service conducted by Lord Radstock,[145] a splendid type of a real Christian gentleman. He had just returned from a visit to the firing line, and this gave pointedness to his splendid and successful appeal to the men to yield themselves to God.

We left K. about midnight on the night of the 17th and travelled in trucks. After making all allowances for the circumstances, it was still a scandal the way we were packed in. About thirty of us travelled in my truck, the centre of which was taken up with officers luggage. We couldn't lay down, or sit with any degree of comfort, the boys at my end having their legs interlocked as they lay. However, when daylight came, we were able to enjoy the scenery, such as it was. I was most

---

145 Lord Radstock, Baron Granville Waldegrave (1859-1937) the 4th Lord Radstock, not to be mistaken for his father, the 3rd Lord Radstock (1833-1913). The 3rd Lord Radstock was a Christian Missionary, especially influential among Russian aristocrats, see David Fountain, *Lord Radstock and the Russian Awakening* (Southampton: Mayflower Christian Books, 1988). He had acquired the Mayfield Estate, Weston, Southampton. His son, Granville, who Philip mentions, encouraged WWI troops and held evangelistic meetings like that described here, and, for example, in David McCasland, *Oswald Chambers: Abandoned to God* (Grand Rapids: Oswald Chambers Publications Association, 1992). Granville was a regular preacher at the Brethren Assembly in Woolston, Southampton, and had close connections with the YMCA.

interested in the railway which represented a wonderful feat of engineering.

The water pipe line about which much has been written ran alongside the railway. By this means, water was run from the Bitter Lakes right up to the front line, thus ensuring water in a barren and waterless desert. As we passed, we could see signs of the previous fighting, especially in the solitary graves of our men. In the early afternoon, we came to El Arish, the oasis of date palms. Here again, a wonderful transformation had been affected, huts and tents abounding everywhere. Huge marquees had been erected for the accommodation of our sick and wounded. About 1.30 p.m. after an exceedingly trying journey, we arrived at Shellal, the then terminus of the line toward Beersheba.

Shellal

A corporal from 181st battery was there to meet us and I was delighted to find he was from the road next to that in which Mother lives. In fact, previous to taking his present house, he had looked over the house where my folk now are. Camels carried our kit for which we were devoutly grateful. After a walk of about two miles, we arrived at our final destination. My first impressions of my new battery were not particularly good ones, but I was very grateful and delighted to come across a Salvation Army soldier who eventually invited me to share his bivouac. In civil life he is a farm labourer, but we had much in common, as all Christians have. I found that the battery was a cockney one, formed almost entirely of men who appeared to have a strange indifference to us draft men. Previous to coming to Egypt, they had served in Salonika where I gathered they had done good work. It fell to my lot to be detailed as a gunner to a gun detachment. We were now not so very far from the firing line, and at night, the flashes and reports of the guns near Gaza were very distinct. It was very hard work at first walking about in the loose sand, but after a while, I got quite used to it.

There is nothing of interest to record about Shellal. It is just a name, for only one house was visible, one owned by a Bedouin farmer. I ought to add here that the soil was very deceptive, for under the sub-soil of sand, there was fine earth, capable of bearing great crops. What I shall have to say later about the possibilities of Palestine applies to these parts.[146]

Our stay at Shellal was by no means a lazy one, for all were busy preparing for our expected early move into the firing line. I had a share in two practice shoots and so managed to in some measure get used to the gun. I found that there was a big difference between the drill at home and the actual practice in the field. I suggest that the civilian tone of the present day army was manifest here, for the drill was just simply used as a means to an end, and adaptable as circumstances required. Surely this is as it should be. Anyhow, the guns were certainly worked far more efficiently and effectively than if the drill had been rigidly adhered to. Furthermore, it afforded scope for individual intelligence and initiative. I therefore really enjoyed the work. A pathetic incident happened during the first march to the firing range. Owing to the exceedingly heavy going, the horses were hard worked, and eventually, a magnificent grey was taken out of our gun team thoroughly exhausted. For some time, it stood, the perspiration literally pouring from its flanks, and eventually it dropped dead, strained to death. It was my first sight of the toll of war, and frankly, it rather upset me. The following day, a Sunday, I was one of a party detailed to bury it, a hard task in the scorching sun.

Here we had our first real experience of the prevalent plague of flies, a plague general to the whole of Egypt and Palestine. Now flies were always my pet aversion, and so I took very badly to their attention for some time. In fact, I never really got used to the feeling of nausea caused by their getting on the food. Not so easily scared as the Blighty varieties, they would hang on to each mouthful of food until actually in the mouth, and one could never really be quite certain that none were eaten. Certainly some were eaten that had got mixed up in

---

146 In the lost Volume.

the food during cooking or while hot. No real peace was possible during the day, for unless covered with a fly net, they kept one busy flicking them off one's face, hands etc. Some of them stung badly and raised irritating sores. The flies too were undoubtedly responsible mainly for the epidemic of septic sores rife everywhere amongst the troops. The least abrasion rapidly developed into a vicious sore, invariably difficult to heal. It was a very common sight "up the line" to see men with hands and arms swathed in bandages, and those who showed no signs of septic sores were few indeed. Later on in the campaign, I had my share of them, and for several weeks both my hands were covered.

Of course, I was interested in all the strange sights seen everywhere. I spent some time watching the big scavenger beetles common to the East. Their sole purpose in life seemed to be to bury every bit of refuse they came across, and wherever and whenever possible, this was usually preceded by the transport of the stuff to where the "Sanitary Orderly" thought fit. This frequently meant removing matter several times heavier than the insect whose strength seemed prodigious.

Interest in the surrounding country was fostered by our Group Padre who used to visit us and talk about the history and geography of the land. We gathered from him that we were then in the Land of the Amalekites.

[Friday 26th October]

On Friday the 26th October, after dumping all private kit, we shifted camp to a spot in the now well known Waddy Ghuzzee,[147] a wide, practically dry river bed, banked by high rocks. One had only to see the place to understand the fierce character of the fighting here. The Turks held commanding positions, and swept all the crossings with murderous machine gun fire.

---

147 Wadi Ghuzzeh.

During the evening, the bombardment Gaza way was intense, a preliminary as it happened to later developments.

Water was scarce here, and each division had its own troughs, fenced with barbed wire and guarded religiously. Unless you could prove that you were entitled to water at any particular place, you couldn't purchase the precious stuff. As units from far off came down here for water, we were able to gather what troops were in front of us. Perhaps the most interesting were the camel cavalry corps, mainly recruited from the Australian and Scottish troops. There was something comic in seeing men of the Scottish Hose, wearing of course thin regimental badges and name plates, mounted on camels. These corps by the way were exceedingly useful, and did fine work until the scene of operations shifted off the desert.

We fast developed into a dirty shirt brigade, for washing facilities were few, and we were on rationed allowance of water.

The evening of Oct 26th saw us on the move to our assigned fighting position, and shortly after leaving the waddy, we struck the Beersheba road. Early as it was, this road, or rather series of parallel roads were packed with all sorts of troops, transport and guns moving up. We found out that Allenby was to spring a surprise upon the Turks, for only outposts and cavalry held the sector we were moving onto, hence the concourse of troops moving up. All along the road were signs of the previous Turkish retreat in the shape of bleached skeletons of horses, mules, bullocks etc. At parts, the track was marked by piles of these bones, a side track being determined by two heaps of bullocks skulls.

We arrived at our position near Abu Shawish at the extreme right of the British line about 2 a.m., and at once began to "dig in", that is, digging gun pits and funk holes.[148] I had been on guard the previous night and so had had very little sleep, therefore I felt very sleepy and was glad to avail myself of an offered chance to drop into the sand for a nap. As you will understand, thought hard over the possibilities of the day

---

148 Holes dug into the sides of pits or trenches to shelter in from bombardment.

ahead, but Psalm 121 recurred to my mind and I felt quite assured and easy in mind and spirit. After less than 2 hrs. sleep, I was awakened, and helped to make final preparations for the bombardment. This commenced as soon as the streaks of dawn were seen in the East. I go "windy" at first, especially as at first I couldn't distinguish between the shells coming overhead from the rear and front. However, the latter were few, and far away, and in a few minutes I was coolly helping to feed our baby[149]. Johnny[150] must have had a terrible shock, for twelve hours previously, not a gun was near this part of his line, and yet at dawn, to my knowledge, three heavy, four siege, and twenty four field batteries were blazing away from a line not more than a mile in length. The Turk concentrated nearly all his artillery on the unfortunate infantry, for, of course, he couldn't fire at batteries in positions he knew nothing about. Furthermore, our aeroplanes prevented any hostile aircraft coming over until late in the day when we were spotted, with however, no evil consequences to us. As the guns were in action the whole day, the detachment was divided into two skeleton detachments, and it fell to my duty on my "shift" to fire the gun. Strangely enough, as I fired, it never occurred to me for some time that I was thus instrumental in discharging death at the enemy, and when I did think of it, I at once felt that after all it was their life or ours, and a sense of competition seized me. You must remember that we were hidden close up under a ridge, and so knew nothing of what we were firing at except when our officer told us. For some time we blazed away at the Turk's trenches. Then a platform of infantry was sent over the top to try and draw the fire of a 5.9[151] battery, the position of which our planes couldn't detect. The ruse succeeded, of course at the cost of the unfortunate infantrymen who were practically annihilated, and our battery was then put on to this enemy battery. We had the huge satisfaction of being told that as the results of good observation and shooting, we knocked out two of the four guns before they could withdraw. We were also told that we had wreaked havoc upon a group of reinforcements. Altogether, we

---

149 Arm the gun with its ammunition.
150 Used to refer to any foreigner by the British, but especially of the Turks in WWI.
151 Reference to the size of shells being fired – 5.9 inches.

earned a good record during the day. Our walking wounded began to stream over about 9 a.m. to the casualty clearing station not far behind us. Please note that. About noon, we were told that Johnny had retreated from a section of his trenches. We helped him. Towards dusk, the retreat became general, and we fired as rapidly as we could. It was hard work, and painful, for my ears were exceedingly sore and each round was as a knife piercing the ear drums. During the afternoon, we saw the first batch of prisoners, a frightened lot. I got a word with one of the guard, a lad of the London Rgt. He said that at first, they had had a rough time, but as soon as our guns got their targets, things went well for them. He was almost comically enthusiastic about the artillery. Just as the daylight began to fail, another big batch of prisoners passed just behind our guns during a temporary lull. We opened fire again just as they were immediately behind us, and their alarm would have been comic if one hadn't remembered what they had experienced before their surrender. In contrast to their fear was the delight of some of our wounded in camel litters[152] who were passing about the same time. In spite of their pain, they cheered us, and yelled "Go on, give 'em 'ell." The total bag of prisoners that day was 1,700. When the light got too bad for observation, we ceased fire, and about 8 p.m. we were ordered to pack up for shifting, and turn in for sleep. My! But I dropped into a dreamless trance straight away. So ended my first day of battle. Needless to add, my last thoughts were of gratitude to God for His preservation and grace.

We slept until about 6 a.m. when we were awakened and ordered to prepare to shift. Johnny had retreated a long way past Beersheba and so we had to move further westward so as to persuade him to continue the movement along his whole line. Accordingly at 9 a.m. We started off on a long tiring march of 10 miles, past some of our concentration trenches.[153] Both men and horses were already feeling the effects of short rations. We had been on a ration of a pint of water per day, our

---

152 A kind of bed/stretcher/saddle designed for carrying the wounded with the assistance of camels.
153 Deeper trenches offering protection from snipers.

privation in this respect being emphasized by our being privileged to behold the officers bathing in the precious fluid. Eventually the horses went 50 hrs. without a drink, and in a desperately hot climate, their work being across loose sand, it is not to be wondered at that they soon showed signs of exhaustion. Arriving at our position, we at once began to dig in and got nicely ready for firing when we were informed that a mistake had been made. The Turkish outposts were just over the ridge with not a single British soldier between. If Johnny had only known, he could have sent a cavalry patrol over and captured the whole lot of us. So much for the intelligence staff of our Group. We therefore made to shift, and we did – in a hurry. The job was a fearfully hard one, for the horses were by now dead beat, and the ground was fearfully difficult for transport. Possibly, few had ever set foot about here, for not only were we well off the tracks, but the ground was quite barren, hilly, and almost impassable for transport except camels, mules etc. We had in part to lower guns and wagons down steep hill sides, and often to come to the aid of the horses and drag everything up slopes. Tired? There ought to be another word coined to fit what we felt like. On every available occasion, we just dropped in our tracks and sometimes dropped sound asleep until shaken into movement again. Finally, the O.C.[154] accepted the obvious and reported we could go no further until the horses had watered, and man and beast had had come rest. Both horses and soldiers looked comic, for the dust and sweat had mixed and we were all caked in white mud. Washing was out of the question since there was no water. Few of us had shaved for three days. Oh! We were a crowd. It was fully 11 p.m. before we got settled down, and I for one immediately died between the blankets and waterproof sheet.[155]

---

154 Officer Commanding.

155 Over the next days, The Group Digest indicates that individual artillery batteries moved independently, and used bivouacs for shelter. A bridge held by the enemy at Samarra and a gun position were targeted by Philip's group. They also engaged an enemy convoy and joined the bombardment in preparation for moving to Beersheba. The Digest says the assault was only made possible due to the heavy bombardment which "silenced the enemy" in spite of aeroplane observations being hampered by low cloud and signals being jammed. *H.A.G Digest 181st Heavy Battery*, The Royal Artillery Museum, Royal Arsenal, Woolwich, London, SE18 6ST.

Nov 2nd

The following day, Nov 2nd, we received orders to leave the guns, the horses and gunners to go back to Karm[156] for a rest, a sensible order for once in a way, for as the horses had to go four miles for a scanty drink, we might just as well go back altogether for a bit. So off we started on what proved to be another diabolical march. The only relieving feature as far as we gunners were concerned was that we were allowed to ride on the spare and "off" horses. Even this was rather a doubtful luxury, for we had no saddles – so got very sore before the long 12 mile march was over. A strong breeze blew the fine dust in our faces and blinded us, horses and men appearing like millers assistants. At every halt many of the horses dropped in their tracks, one dying. En route, we had a treat however, for we halted at a huge well, one existent in patriarchal days and probably used by the wandering Israelites. We were allowed to drink our fill, and only those who had been rationed as we had been can appreciate with what abandon we drank. This was my first real unlimited drink since I left Alexandria. The character of the country through which we passed was evidenced by the plentiful remains of horses etc. everywhere. Eventually we arrived at our destination half impotent from fatigue. One really marvelled at the power of human endurance for in addition to the driving dust, and the fearful "going", the heat was terrific.

The following day, I had to report sick with an injured back, the result of the strain of hauling the guns. There was a fairly large sick parade, and when we set off for the medical tent, we had only a very hazy idea where to go to. I might add here, that we had no first aid conveniences in the battery, and very often we were far removed from any medical or surgical help if anything serious had happened to any one of us. The flying dust acted as a fog, and we wandered aimlessly around for about two hours and then gave the job up and returned to

---

156 Between Gaza and Beersheba.

camp. Some of the men could scarcely crawl, two of them being badly weakened by prolonged diarrhoea. We got no sympathy on our return, the N.C.O in charge being "choked off"[157] for returning before finding a dressing station. The officer in charge then sent off an orderly after a doctor and eventually brought back a specimen who ought not have the medical supervision of pigs. He gave a supercilious glance at each of us, gave us some pills, no matter what the complaint, and ordered us to carry on our duties. It was no use complaining for the powers that were, were quite indifferent. Later on I shall have something to record about our officers and NCOs.

An interesting sight hereabouts was the huge dumps. These formed one of the marvels of organisation out here. Huge mounds of forage, biscuits, wood, bully beef, cheese, bacon etc. stored on acres of ground. As a general rule, these dumps were near the railway but in certain spots, all the produce was brought up by camels. It is impossible to say how much of the successful organisation was due to these ships of the desert. The government had commanded all they could get, and several thousand were used on all sorts of jobs, carrying rations, water, material, and litters for the sick and wounded. The desert campaign would have been almost impossible without these, and one wonders how Napoleon and others managed in their desert marches, although it must be remembered that the width of their fields of operations was confined to the coast, and little fighting took place between the borders of Egypt and Palestine. On the coast, the dumps were often supplied from ships by means of native boats, and when the line moved well up into Judea, these ships brought practically all the produce which was, after unloading, put on to trains and so carried to the forward dumps. The method of distribution would have startled the ordinary civilian purveyor. The A.S.C.[158] orderlies became adept at guessing quantities, and would hack off a meat ration, shovel out tea and sugar, split cheeses, divide sacks of potatoes and other vegetables, throw sides of bacon about, and so on with uncanny celerity and accuracy. But although we often had

157 Rebuked.
158 Army Service Corps.

plenty of food to eat, especially when at rest anywhere, we were always glad of the canteen, whenever we could get to one to purchase additions to our supplies. Hence at Karm, I made a good Sunday dinner off bully and a big tin of pork and beans, tea being made somewhat sabbathic by the acquisition of a cake.

At Karm, I was again thrown into the company of my Christian pal, and he and I had some helpful chats together. Oh how precious these chats were. No matter how close a communion one may enjoy with God, one always felt the need of an exchange of thought, ideas and experiences.

After a two days rest, we moved off back again to the guns. Fortunately the wind had dropped somewhat, so that our return journey was not so bad as the other. After picking up the guns again, we moved off N.E. for about 5 miles, getting into position about 3 a.m. Of course, that meant another sleepless night, for we only finished preparing for action about an hour before dawn, when we opened fire on the end of the Turkish line that had not followed the retreat of those at Beersheba. We fired for about 3 hrs. and then hurriedly packed up and went forward another 2,000 yards to assist the Turk to continue the retreat he had started about an hour previously. On our way, we passed the enemy forward trenches, an interesting feature of which was the praying stools. These were flat topped circular mounds about 2'6" in diameter, the top being rather prettily decorated with inlaid stones, fixed to various patterns. We were now right in the line of attack, and infantry moved up past us in platoons as reinforcement to the attacking troops. Occasionally, a body of prisoners passed us to the rear, conspicuous by their dirty and ragged appearance. The general colour scheme of their uniform was field grey, but many of them appeared to be dressed in whatever they had succeeded in picking up to take the place of their worn out uniform. The military scheme here was to try and make a gap in the enemy lines so as to permit an attack on Gaza, 20 miles distant, from the east. After another two hours shoot, we again moved forward along the line of our advance. Owing to the exigencies of the work, we had not time for cooking and had to eat our food as best we could, and as we were again on a water ration of 1 pint, we had a rough time of it. But we cared little for this, for we were advancing and that made any privation well worth while. Furthermore, we knew we were driving towards wells and so felt we had a definite object in view. Johnny's artillery tried to find us, but he guessed badly. Just before dusk, we made another move forward about a mile and prepared again for action the following morning. The Turk had by now retreated about five miles to prearranged positions, and managed to stay any further advance by our troops.

[Nov 7th]

At dawn the following day, Nov 7th, we found ourselves on ground fought over the day before, and dead men and discarded kit lay in all directions. The Kensington Rifles were the chief sufferers, and close to my gun lay the body of a young lad shot through the head. By the way, steel helmets had not up to then been served out to the troops in Egypt, and if this lad had been wearing one, it would have stopped the shot that killed him. Later on in the day we dug a grave and buried him. The reverence of our lads was splendid, and they did what they could to make the grave ornamental. We opened fire early, and again were in the direct line of attack. For about three hours, the enemy held on to his ground, and then an attack was pushed home and the Turk cleared out. Impetus was given to the troops' work by the news during the morning that Gaza had been captured. What this meant to the infantry may be understood from what the lads who were in last April's failure said about that "regrettable incident." That afforded only one of innumerable instances on this and other fronts where the incompetency of our leaders had to be paid for with the lives of hundreds of brave lads. Gaza was then actually taken, but owing almost entirely to the fact that the G.O.C.[159] General Murray was at Cairo from where he conducted the campaign, and so far removed from the scene of operations, the victory was turned

159 General Officer Commanding.

into a defeat. I knew of lads at Alex. who cried over the blunder. In contrast to the above, Gen Allenby always kept well up near the fighting line and his subsequent success was no doubt in part due to this. Our stint was now going well, and about 3 p.m., we were out of range and so had to make another move forward. But Johnny was now retreating rapidly and we only managed to get four rounds into him from the new position before he was again out of range. It was now useless for the time being for us to try and follow up the advance, so we stayed where we were and managed to get a badly needed rest.

I seized the chance to shave a three days growth off with the aid of a small portion of tea saved over from dinner.

Early next morning, our officer told us that the fight had gone so well, that our troops had captured the desired wells intact. This resulted in an order to the effect that we could now have as much water as we liked. Needless to add, we liked and got a lot. We had an alarm during the morning when the enemy counter attacked some miles away, but this was squashed and eventually we were told that the retreat had gone 10 miles from the positions occupied 24hrs. previously. This meant for us, no further shooting here, and so we just "lazied" around and tried to make up for arrears of rest and sleep. That evening I was on guard and so had another of those opportunities always prized of a nocturnal talk with the Friend.

The following day about 11.30 a.m., we were on the move again, and striking eastward, we crossed the Gaza – Beersheba railway near Tel-el-Sheria, an important junction. The fighting here had been exceedingly desperate, and dead men, horses and mules lay in all directions, and so thick that it was only with care that our teams managed to escape running over some of them. A big pumping station was the prize fought for and this was captured quite intact. I must here record that I know of no single instance during the whole of my active service where the Turks poisoned the wells etc. Of course, occasionally he did destroy the pumps and gears but that is quite legitimate. This practice of the "Unspeakable Turk"[160] affords a striking contrast to the usual conduct of the gentle, cultured, Hun.[161] A single hill, or rather mound stood near the station, and this had been defended to the last by a party of heroic Turks. The outcome of this was seen in the scores of dead of both sides lying round about. Some of the corpses lay in a stream, and the water was a ghastly sight. I am rather tempted to describe more fully the horrors of this spot, not to harrow your feelings, but because judging by what one reads, and the pictures one sees in the illustrated papers of Battlefield scenes, pictures which no edition dare have published four years ago, I fancy that the horror of war is no longer understood I felt as it was. Susceptibilities are blunted, and the finer scenes dulled. Glories of war? Yes perhaps in individual exploits of bravery, but war as a whole, as a scheme is indescribably hellish, and I assert that no soldier who has actually seen war in all its naked horror will ever again detect anything of glory in it. As I write, I think of the pitiful sights I've seen, the flower of manhood, made carrion, disfigured, dehumanised. Oh yes, I am mindful of the purpose for which they died, the holy war in which they fought, and if war were inevitable and the only way to secure these aims, I should gladly, if sadly agree that it were all worth while. But is it the only way, is it inevitable? I saw some of the lads pass our guns on their way forward, the perfection of physical manhood, the pardonable delight of mother, wife or sweetheart, and now? Yes they still hold the pride of place and the place of pride, but the horror of it all! Oh I'm a rotten soldier, I think, and no soldier should think. After all, I shall never be more than a mere camouflaged civilian. I wish for no greater punishment for those who delight in war than that they should see the issue of their purposes, taste its horrors, share its privations, feel its hell. But there – this is a record, not a treatise or essay. The stench at Sheria was awful, and to add to the nausea one felt, swarms of flies varied their resting places with no nice distinctions. Beyond the station were the remains of a big Turkish hospital and a huge dump. These both had been partly

---

160 Derogatory term for reputed Turkish brutality.
161 The Germans to whom Turkey was allied.

destroyed, but the dump still contained hundreds of pounds worth of valuable material. As soon as possible, the lads got busy on a souvenir hunting stint, and many of us gathered stuff which alas, we soon had to discard in the interests of mobility. I here saw for the first time, samples of that typical weapon of the civilised Hun, the sword bayonet. I guess however, that was not used much out here. We managed to find a spot in the waddy stream, uncontaminated by corpses, and we had the satisfaction of seeing our animals drink their fill. It was ticklish work leading them to the water, for no sooner did they see it than they rushed to slake their thirst.

We were in a queer position the next day, for owing to the rapidity of the advance, we had got too far ahead of supplies, and so started the day with no food except the very limited emergency rations. The horses were put on ¼ rations, and we ourselves had only one biscuit, and about 2ozs of bully beef to last us until we could get supplies up. It came as no surprise therefore, when in view of the distance the enemy was now away from us, and the fact of food shortage, that we were ordered on a two days march back to Karm again. As we repassed the sumps, we saw groups of Bedouins collecting clothing, flour, and articles of domestic value, and guess that they at least were glad of Johnny's homeward trek. These Bedouins, who abound throughout Palestine were typical of their race, and clearly descendants of Ishmael. I have read that they never marry outside their tribe and therefore have kept right down the ages, their purity of stock. True nomads, they never settle anywhere for long, and even in Palestine proper, they stay at any one place, only long enough to raise crops or land that seems to belong to anyone who cares to cultivate it. On the desert, they live in camel hair tents, which conform in style and arrangement exactly to what is pictured in Scripture, e.g. the tents of Kedar mentioned in Canticles.[162]

Our route lay along the Turkish line of retreat and across loose sand, and bad as previous marches had been, this was the

---

162 Also called Song of Solomon, or Song of Songs. 1:5 "Dark am I, yet lovely, O daughters of Jerusalem, dark like the tents of Kedar, like the tent curtains of Solomon."

worst. We had to reach a certain place by a certain hour, hence halts were few and short, and the pace was the quickest possible. Then too, we were marching on practically empty stomachs and as we only had what water we carried in our bottles, we felt the scorching heat more than we otherwise should have done. True, it was only an 8 mile march, but a walk of 28 miles at home wouldn't have affected us as this did. By the time we got to Abu Irgig[163] our halt, we were quite "down and out." After unhooking, the horses had to go another 5 miles before they could get a drink.

Wisely, the guns, ammunition wagons and heavy baggage was left behind under guard when we set off early the following morning. This not only allowed the horses to travel light, but gave us gunners a chance to ride, and although many like myself felt very sore when we got to the end of this 10 mile march to Karm, we were grateful for the change. A third class ride is invariably better than a first class walk. But a dust storm proved the acme of discomfort and right glad were we when at last we got to our destination. It was Sunday, but I failed to sense a sabbathic blessing. I am a very long way off Paul's achievement, when he could say "I have learned, in whatsoever state, to be content."[164] The grace was there, but not the grasp. I felt very cheerless until the arrival of a mail, and then the temperamental thermometer went up to summer heat. Oh! Those blessed mails. How often have they proved an uplift, a cheer and a blessing.

We enjoyed our stay here, for we got bread, a welcome change from hard tack[165], a real rest and a canteen. My first purchase was a tin of fruit and a bob's worth of toffee.

I have already written enough regarding our life out here to enable you to realise that we were not, as sometimes imagined at home, on a picnic. Very few of the comforts obtainable in France ever came our way, and except for two or three supplies of books, we never benefited by any of the

---

163 ? Abu Irgeig Approx. 5 miles NW of Beersheba.
164 Philippians 4:11.
165 A kind of tasteless hard biscuit.

numerous "comforts funds" operating in England. Y.M.C.As etc., canteens and recreation huts were very rarely seen up the line, and even the canteens were only moderately stocked. Even allowing for exaggerated feelings due to present experiences, there was something in the remarks of those who had fought there "Give me France any old day."

We might have been much more comfortable here if the officers had been more considerate. Other units near us fared much better than we did. For instance, we still suffered from a shortage of water. It only required fetching in the water carts from the railway. We had to look on and see other units washing shirts etc. and having a real good tubbing, while we ourselves could get scarcely enough to drink and wash our faces. An extra supply of water was once procured to wash the harness with. On joining the battery, I soon was told what sort of officers and NCOs we had got. The men even had to shift[166] for themselves, and even their extras such as rum, cigarettes and tobacco, and candles were frequently sequestrated. In Salonika, during the depth of a Balkan winter when the men were half froze and a rum issue a god send, the sergeants were frequently drunk on the rum they had robbed the troops of. Complaints were quite useless, and were sometimes met with penalties inflicted on the complainant. The same thing happened if the food were not up to the mark. We just had to put up with it. The cursing of the officers was vile, and here again, no complaint availed unless one was prepared to take it to the Colonel of the Group to which we belonged, for the Major was as bad as the rest, and even if taken to the Colonel, one could always be certain of victimisation. I am very hot-tempered in the matter of being swore at and fortunately, I rarely met with this personally. And so it may be realised how much our hardships were added to as the result of this.

Part of the time we were at Karm, I had a bivouac to myself for my chum had to go to hospital suffering from a severe cold. I enjoyed the privacy and was able to get some real blessed seasons with God in prayer, and Bible reading. At this

---

166 Used to mean "look after" or provide for their own needs in this context.

place too, we had the privilege of Sunday services, the CofE[167] padre being a fine evangelical preacher. During our rest, I was also able to clear off arrears of correspondence, no small job. One bit of news from home came somewhat as a shock, and that was respecting the death of Father. But here I couldn't feel sad even if I wanted to, for Dad knew God as his Father and Friend, and to him, death was a glorious release from a life the latter part of which was one of the acutest kind of suffering. Nay, I rejoiced over the Christian hope, that they in Christ who pass away, pass straight into the presence of the King, Whose life is theirs, and in Whom is eternal joy, rest and peace. Certainly, Dad seems nearer now than ever before, and Heaven itself as the homeland of which earth is but as a colony, or as halting place en route.

One very interesting sight we saw one day was a train load of captured Turkish guns. All of these had been made in Germany and Austria, and one felt some satisfaction in having taken part in reducing pro tem at least the number of guns serviceable against our lads.

An inconvenience was the desperately cold nights. We had only one blanket each and this with the top coat was our only covering. After dark, we felt cold about the knees, for we only had thin short knickers on.

A couple of days before we struck camp, the guns were brought in, so that when on Nov 29th we left under orders to march northwards, we were a full battery. The first march was one of 8 miles to one of the outer defences of Gaza, Reita[168] redoubt, a powerful obstruction to our advance which was eventually taken from the rear after we had pushed the Turk beyond Sheria, part of our troops wheeling to a flank for this purpose. It was my first view of a modern gun redoubt and I was keenly impressed by the skill employed in making such defences. This particular one would be impervious to anything

---

167 Church of England.
168 Hard to decipher spelling. There were a number of strong redoubts stretching between Gaza and Beersheba, including Hureira/Hareira, the most likely mentioned here, since it is approx. 8 miles north of Karm as described.

less than an 8 inch shell weighing about 200 lbs, and could safely and successfully defy a frontal infantry attack. We were now nearing the edge of the desert, and the ground was therefore firmer, a welcome relief after the loose sand. After pitching camp, I was provided with an opportunity to display my first aid ability, one of our drivers having been thrown off his horse and badly bruised. I soon discovered no bones were broken, but after dressing the wounds and generally massaging his body, I suggested sending for a medical officer, and he, when he arrived promptly packed the man off to hospital.

After reveille at 4 a.m. we had breakfast, and was on the way towards Gaza at 7 a.m. Our way lay past the outer defences of this city, and one could quite realise that Gaza was "a strong place" indeed. In spite of our heavy artillery fire, the trench systems were still in a good condition and the taking of them was only at a big price. One big redoubt was known as Tank Redoubt, one of our tanks, used in the April operations coming to grief there, the crew being captured and the tank converted into an additional defence. The ground around here was packed with shell holes, the efforts to demolish the tank being unsuccessful. A distinct belt of "No mans [sic] land" was evidenced by the gruesome skeletons lying around. Many of these were quite indistinguishable as to which side they belonged to, even the uniforms being rotted beyond recognition. At this redoubt, I had the pleasure of meeting a number of lads who came out from England with me. They belonged to a siege battery near by, that had played no small part in the attack on Gaza. The roads now were quite hard and soon the feet of the gunners got very sore, mine being blistered badly. The countryside was now pastoral, and flocks were grazing everywhere. Even a novice could appreciate the boundless possibilities of the soil, and under a proper system of irrigation and cultivation, this district might well become rich and fertile. After the monotonous landscape of the desert, we enjoyed the fresh view, and were keenly interested in the varying forms of pastoral life. We, to our regret passed to the west of Gaza, and as it is bordered by hills, on the other side of which lay our route, we had no chance of seeing this city of

Philistia.[169] We were now over the border line and in Palestine proper, and although we had the prospect of hard work in front of us, we were right delighted to get away from the wearisome desert.

Part III In Judea

En route, we were glad to be able to purchase oranges from the numerous hawkers. Of course, we had no idea at first of the value of these, and my first purchase was at the rate of 3 for 1 piastre, but eventually we got 6 fine oranges for the same amount. My! But we gorged ourselves, for fruit was indeed a luxury. We came to a halt after a 15 mile tramp, at a mud village 5 miles beyond Gaza. Oh but we were glad to get there, for I for one was so badly crippled that walking was exceedingly painful. When I got my socks off, they were well discoloured with blood. In the ordinary way of course, such a walk would never have bothered us, but coming off the soft sand, the hard roads worked havoc upon our feet. Our camp was pitched near the road, one of the five great Roman roads in Palestine. Shell holes were everywhere, and here and there lay "dud" unexploded shells, two huge 12" shells, fired from monitors[170] at sea lying uninvitingly near our lines. We were now on historic ground, a part of the wide plain of Philistia, and judging by my map, I gathered that a big village to the east would be Gath.[171] Deir Seneid near by is an important railway junction and was, when we passed it, a point of concentration for several Army departments.

On Sat Dec 1st, the day following, we were on the march again about 9.30 a.m. and right glad were we foot sloggers that

169 Note the intentional use of the Bible term, rather than the usual usage of "Palestine" as in the next statement.
170 Shallow draught ships carrying one or two large guns.
171 Famously where Goliath came from.

it was only a short walk of 5 miles. We travelled along one of the five great Roman roads of Palestine, the new railway a two tracked one running nearly parallel to this. The Turk metre gauge railway was almost intact, and a fair amount of enemy rolling stock was running over it as we passed. But most of the rail traffic was over the British broad gauge track which had been laid in a surprisingly quick time. Huge piles of captured Turk ammunition lay everywhere; the small arm stuff being of Turkish manufacture and the heavy stuff German and Austrian. An amusing incident occurred when some of our lads on passing a flock of sheep undertook to try and purchase one for dinner. The little lad in charge at first thought we were intent on commandeering the flock, but when at last he understood what was wanted, he offered to give them away. One was eventually bought @ 5 piastres, a shilling!! One noticeable sight was the heavily laden donkeys and camels used by the natives. Both these beasts are used by our army out here, the permissible weights for them to carry being very much less than these poor beasts we saw were carrying. We halted at a big village, Beit Ejje,[172] and I was grateful to be able to get my boots off and to hop around in a pair of Turkish sandals I had picked up. During the bright moonlight night Johnny Turk made an air raid on Deir Seneid station and of course, put the wind up us. Most of our fellow had been through both shell fire and air raids, and were unanimously agreed that an air attack is far and away the most unnerving. Speaking for myself, I never properly lost my head during a hot time of any sort except once, and that was during an air raid. I think this is due to the fact that after a little experience, one can tell fairly accurately by the sound it makes when approaching, where a shell will fall, and so if circumstances permit, can dodge for cover, but no-one can tell where a dropping bomb will land.

We made our early start next day and were well on our way by 7 a.m. The road runs about 3 miles east of Askelon,[173] and from the point where this town of the Philistines was

---

172 Could refer to a number of villages west of Gath and 10 to 15 miles NE. of Gaza. ?
   Modern town of Ge'a.
173 Ashkelon.

visible we could see the sea, so near and yet so far. The country hereabouts was interesting, crops of sugar corn abounding everywhere. An interesting sight too were the mud villages. I had no chance of seeing the interior of any one of the huts, but I surmised from the outward shape that they are similar to those I saw in India; if so, they would be comfortable and clean. Julius[174] and El Sawafir,[175] were big specimens of those which we passed. We noticed that the retreating Turk had wrought havoc with the railway about here, and almost every bridge and culvert had been destroyed and scores of yards of line removed. The roads too were badly damaged, but gangs of Egyptian Labour Corps were at work on both rail and road. Long strings of red cross cars passed us carrying wounded down south, some of the lads sitting with the drivers appearing very badly exhausted and in some cases, smothered with blood. My feet were now so bad, that after going a few miles I had to ask for a ride, but as the road was so fearfully rough and riding such a torture, I was glad to get down again and hobble along in rear of the column. By gum! It was an 18 mile penance. But it was a case of "sticking it," for no relief was possible. Just before we got to Yasur, our halt, we climbed a hill from the top of which we got a very fine surprise view of the Valley of Sorek, of Samson fame, stretching away to the north west. The countryside was cultivated in plots, the various colours having a kaleidoscopic effect under the moving rays of the sun. Very noticeable amongst these patches were those cultivated by the Jews, whose colonies here were the first we saw. I shall have more to say about the Jewish colonies later. A fine rock village, Abu Esh, lay well over on our right. After halting, we watered our horses at a village well. The big demand for water by the British troops made it necessary to ration the natives, British guards being placed over the wells, and water issued to the natives at certain hours. This must have fallen rather hard on the natives, but they got a fairly liberal allowance and were in any case better off than when the Turks were about, for they willy nilly took

---

174 Julis.
175 Al Sawafir or Es Suafir 5 miles SE of Ashdod.

whatever they wanted without any regard to the requirements of the natives.

We only did four miles the following day, quite enough for me and others whose feet were sore. My big difficulty was not so much taking the boots off as putting them on, for the feet were so badly swollen and sore, that this operation was an agony. We were now near the western foothills of the Judean hills, and I felt conscious of being on historic ground.

The next stage of our journey was one of 5 miles to Naaneh,[176] and here we rested for 6 days. Near by was The Junction, where three lines met. It was an important place, so much so that not only had the enemy destroyed what he could of the track, but he made frequent air raids to prevent our people repairing the damage early. Not until our aeroplanes managed to gain the ascendancy over their rivals did the work progress, and then huge dumps of stones were made. Much amusement and interest was caused by the sight of a mixed ploughing team at work consisting of an ox and a camel. If unmatched as regards size, they certainly were well matched as regards pace, a slow one, for oxen and camels travel at about the same pace when in draught. The rest at Naaneh was welcome in more senses than one, for the halt allowed us to get our feet well again and to wash our filthy bodies and clothing. The arrival of a mail added to the sense of refreshment, for a mail is always a reviver. In this connection, I was rather badly hit however by the news received of the death of my Blighty chum, Harry Jackson, in France. We both hoped at home that we should succeed in keeping together during our service and it was a disappointment when we were separated. It was a keen satisfaction to remember that Harry was known of his Lord and Master, and that his death in action was the entry into the longer life where his talent will have full play and scope. Young as he was, he was old in his experience of the saving and keeping grace of God, and the sense of loss was tempered by the knowledge that he is now with the King whom he loved and served so well. By the way, he fell on Oct 10th, the news

---

176 Modern Na'an, previously Al Na'ani.

reaching me on Dec 4th. From this you will understand that we all felt the distance that separated us from loved ones at home, to be, not so much a matter of distance as of time. We were two, sometimes three, always at least one month's journey from home and the thought of what might happen in that time always brought a feeling of anxiety. I know the home folk felt the same.

My birthday (Dec 5th) fell on the day following our arrival at Naaneh, and I spent the best part of the day as one of a party on a well improvement fatigue,[177] This village well at which we watered was typical of many such all over Palestine. The well proper measured about 10 feet across. Over the well and through an opening in the arched roof was suspended an endless chain of wooden box shaped buckets, one part of which ran under the water and the opposite part over a wheel. At the end of the axle of this wheel was another double wheel the two outsides rims of which were joined together by a number of horizontal pegs. These pegs in their turn engaged in a number of upright pegs fixed in another large wheel which was fastened on the top of a pivotal post. In this post again was inserted a long pole, and to this pole was fastened the animal which walked in a circle around the post. The water ran out of the buckets at the top through a wooden channel and along a groove in the stonework to a large stone tank from which the water could be run as required. This type of well is, I believe, as was common in the days of the patriarchs. It was the "walk" which we had to "improve" as we found it deep in mud. This we did by the placing of loads of stones. As it started raining while we were on the job, it was not a very pleasant way of spending a birthday. Both the well and the village were undamaged. It was interesting to watch the groups of natives, and a village parliament presided over by an elderly sheikh was worth seeing. The camping ground had two big drawbacks, one being the profusion of "Pontius Pilate" thorns, and the clayey character of the soil. When it rained, as it did, hard, during our stay, the ground became fearfully soft and horrible. Inside the "bivvys" soon became wet and soft, and even if the bed became

---

177 A non-military assignment like digging.

a little less hard, the dampness gave us all sore joints. As this was our last halt before going into action again, we were kept constantly on the qui vive awaiting orders to move. The conditions were exceedingly cheerless and yet the lads kept so wonderfully cheerful that I thought, "What a lesson to many Xians,[178] P.B. included." I found it constantly necessary to flee to my Refuge for grace to "stick it" and many good times I had in communion with the Friend.

On Dec 10th we got orders to move off and accordingly packed up and started off about 2 p.m. We only travelled a matter of about 200 yds and then most of the transport got stuck in the thick mud. It took us 2 hrs. to get our gun going, and then only with the aid of several extra horses taken off some wagons which had got through to Ramleh.[179] When we got outside Ramleh about 1.15 a.m., we got so badly stuck as to be unable for the time being to get any further. All the blankets, coats etc. belonging to we gunners were on an ammunition wagon, which had got well ahead. This meant that we were stranded without any other covering than our thin drill clothing to withstand the cold that got pretty severe. I nearly forgot to mention that just before dusk, we were travelling along a lane so narrow, that there was no room for other traffic to pass us. Accordingly a number of camels travelling toward us had to climb to the top of a steep bank by the road side. As the gun passed some of these, two of them slid down the slippery bank side and in some inexplicable fashion got their legs clear under the gun between the front and rear wheels. Fortunately the horses stopped dead before the wheels caught the legs of the struggling camels. The European N.C.O. in charge of the camels had the good sense to leave the task of extricating the beasts, to their native drivers, and after a struggle, these managed to get their charges clear. As may be realised, our condition outside Ramleh soon became decidedly unpleasant for in addition to having no warm coverings, we were without food. A good Samaritan in the shape of an A.S.C.[180] motor driver

---

178 Christians.
179 Modern town is called Ramla.
180 Army Service Corps.

who was camped near by, supplied us with hot tea and bully beef and biscuits, otherwise we should have felt the cold more than we did. Our horses were taken out of the gun and sent on ahead, and eventually, horses were sent back to fetch the gunners, the gun being left as it stood. All except one gun and its accompanying ammunition wagons which had gone ahead to try and get into the firing position by daylight, we found camped about 2 miles beyond Ramleh. Our way there lay for awhile along a lane, the water in which was up to the horses bellies. The marvel was that any traffic at all got through there. Only a couple of hours were left for sleep, and my Xian chum lent me a blanket which I rolled around me and then dropped down on the wet ground and shivered until daybreak. The muddy lane near us was in an indescribable condition. Not only was the mud about 18 inches deep, but the road was broken and uneven, an awful place to travel along by day, and yet traffic had passed over it at night. We found that one of our ammunition wagons had come to grief, being completely overturned and resting bottom uppermost. The gun which had gone forward came to grief the other side of Lud.[181] It ran off the narrow road when going round a corner, and rolled clean down an embankment into a ditch 20 feet below. It took a couple of infantry companies to get it out the following day. It will thus be seen that the attempt to get into position failed completely. What this meant was evidenced later the next day when we saw our infantry badly battered in a counter attack in front of Lud. Our four guns would probably have scotched Johnny Turk and saved scores of casualties amongst our lads. We set off about 5 p.m. again to try and get into position, our gun meanwhile having been brought up from Ramleh. Passing through Lud after dark, we succeeded, after travelling over rivers of mud in getting into the appointed positions about midnight. Dead beat as we were, we had of course to dig in, no light job in the hard rocky soil. Again we only had about 2 hrs for sleep, and again we were without coat or blanket, for our wagon had been passed in the dark near Lud and had not reached the firing line. Gee! But it was cruelly cold and although I got under a heavy

---

181 Modern town called Lod.

123

tarpaulin and slept on a bed of shells with cartridges for a pillow, I was frozen to the bone.

Our position was about 14 miles dead west of Jerusalem and between two hill villages Jindas and Dia Rhea.[182] Although no mention was made of it, I fancy a mistake had been made, for although near the trenches, we never fired a shot from here, and two days later we got into a fresh spot about 3,000 yds further along the ravine. In both positions we were visited by natives selling bread, native tobacco and oranges. The bread was black, but tasty and so long as one didn't question in the mind how and where it was baked, was fairly appetising. For some reason or other the tobacco ration had fallen off and as we were far away from canteens, the only smokes we could get was this vile "Gippo" tobacco. In connection with the purchas [sic] of goods from the natives, they quoted in shillings and never gave change for notes. The high prices charged was the result of the readiness of the Australians with their higher pay to give what was asked of them. This was always a real grievance everywhere and created a lot of discontent and grumbling amongst the British troops. Certainly, the British soldier is underpaid as compared with the civilian worker who serves in safety, but there should surely be a standard rate of pay for all classes of soldiers, and if the British rate is a 1/- per day, why pay the Australian 6/-? There is every proof that prices everywhere were three and four times higher than they would have been but for the "Dinkums." The refusal of the natives to give change was twofold. They thereby made more money for a man would buy 50 piastres worth of stuff when he would otherwise have bought say 10pt worth only. Also, the natives were not conversant with our coinage and so solved the difficulty by dealing only with currency they understood.

Aeroplanes bothered us in this last position and it was amusing to see our "old man" get the wind up. His Salonique[183] experiences had raised his fears, and if an enemy aeroplane hove[184] into sight, woe betide any unfortunate who moved until

---

182 Possibly Al-Duhayriyya!
183 Salonika.
184 Heaved.

the "all clear" whistle sounded. Spies were numerous here, and daily, some of these passed us, escorted by Military Police en route to Lud and the bullet. There is little doubt that our position was discovered to the enemy by some of these gentry, as events proved. While here, we had our first rum issue and I gladly accepted mine. Oh! Please don't get shocked my tetotal[sic] friends. I made no excuse for drinking this, for no excuse I hold necessary. All honour to those who from principle refused their rum ration. I personally never took the rum ration unless I felt it would do me good, and when, as was often the case, I was wet through and shivering from cold, I never argued with myself as to its efficacy, but drank and was grateful. I respectfully submit that anyone who bids to blame me or anyone for accepting the rum ration is not in a position to judge, as they cannot adequately appreciate the exact circumstances under which it was received.[185]

[Dec 15th]

On Sat Dec 15th, a general attack was made in front of us, and we opened out at 8 a.m. On a long strafe. We were packed up tight under a ridge and so quite free from enemy observation and yet Johnny searched consistently for us. He knew from his spies we were there. Shells fell fast to our left front, a big German colony, Wilhelma catching it severely. Another village, Beit Neballa[186] near to us was early in ruins, the Turk evidently surmising we had observation posts there. As a matter of fact our battery O.P.s[187] were in our front line trenches. The gun position was near the end of a ridge of hills, from the end of which stretched a big plain, and it was on this that so many of Johnny's shells fell. It caused us excitement to see convoys and transport and single horsemen at the full

---

185 During this time, the 181st Battery had joined the 100th Heavy Artillery Group, headquartered at Lud. They "assisted" the enemy retreating, in spite of the terrible weather. *H.A.G Digest 181st Heavy Battery,* The Royal Artillery Museum, Royal Arsenal, Woolwich, London, SE18 6ST.
186 Bayt Nabala.
187 Observation Posts.

gallop pursued by shrapnel shells. We saw no casualties however. The Turks retreated a little on the first attack, but during the whole day successfully resisted further attacks until nightfall when after a tornado of shell, he left our lads in possession of his tunnel system and retreated to his support trenches..

After nightfall, one of our men conceived the idea of erecting a shelter big enough to accommodate the whole of the detachment, and as my own "bivvy" was erected on ground covered with sharp "Pontius Pilate" thorns, I though it best to "muck in" with the rest. So we commandeered a big tarpaulin and after some difficulty due to the high wind and the character of the ground, managed to erect a shelter. I however found that I was out of the frying pan into the fire, for the ground was so uneven and stony, that an even bed was quite impossible. However, I managed to somehow arrange a plot for myself, and got fairly comfortably settled when a peg near my head came up and I was nearly smothered under the weight of the "sheet". Out I crawled and fastened the peg in again, but only temporary for out it came again. I then decided I would try and "stick it" as it was, and finally succeeded in getting off to sleep. But not for long, for a passing wagon got too close in the darkness to our "tent" with the result that a wheel ran over one of the guide ropes, which pulled away a support, and brought the whole affair tumbling down upon us. The tarpaulin was too heavy to sleep under, so cold as it was, I just dragged out my bed as it was and with a prayer that it wouldn't rain during the night, got again between the blankets and slept until daybreak.

Early the following morning we got the wind up through hostile aircraft flying low down over our position, with the result that shells fell on the ridge not very far in front of us. I often wondered why Johnny was not more daring and enterprising with his planes, for I do not know of a single occasion when he had an aeroplane shoot on any battery, whereas that was a daily feature with us. The only reason I can think of is that he had too few planes to risk unduly the destruction of any, and he certainly had a very wholesome respect for our fliers. Certainly, he could have very quickly shot us clean off the landscape had he risked the necessary observation. Here I may mention, that during the whole of the campaign out here, it appeared to be the praiseworthy aim of our generals to always secure if possible, the points of observation before suspending an advance; and if by any chance, a halt should leave Johnny with any useful observation points, to attack and capture these before "digging in". Therefore we were invariably in positions quite hidden from direct observation.

Our big privation here was the shortage of smoking materials, for most of us including myself had grown used to the weed. Now and again it was possible to buy the ration muck, but as the vendors refused to give change for notes, and as the lowest value in notes we had was 50 piastres, it meant buying 10/- worth at a time if we wanted any. Some of the men solved the difficulty by drying the tea leaves after tea was brewed and smoked that. One afternoon in company with another of our detachment, I went to Lud and there we spent £1 in the purchase of bread, native tobacco and cigarette papers. This afforded me a chance of looking around the Jewish colony in Lud.

The Jewish Colony of Ben Shemen is an experimental station, a part of the Jewish Colonisation Scheme where experiments were made in dairy farming, poultry farming, cultivation and preservation of fodder etc. The chief was an American Jew, and his native shrewdness and American ingenuity was evidence in the up-to-date and cleverly schemed arrangements. It was said that the plant, buildings, produce, fields etc. represented an original outlay of £20,000, and I could well believe that. Every available piece of ground was utilised and in passing through the farm, I saw amongst other things, a line of intensive poultry sheds, apiaries, well ordered vegetable gardens, orchards, vineyards, olive groves, eucalyptus groves, up to date cattle sheds, modern irrigation plant and systems, in fact, a veritable model farm. I have subsequently read that the results in various directions obtained here have been of the highest value to Jewish colonies elsewhere. The workmen were accommodated in pretty bungalows grouped around the central farm dwellings. I must add that both the Turk and the British had taken heavy toll of the produce etc. but except for an oil refinery nearby, I saw nothing damaged badly. There were few men about however, for those of enemy extraction had been removed by our people. A few days after my visit, Johnny shelled the farm with a long range gun and killed fourteen and badly damaged some of the buildings. This was undoubtedly due to the fact that our artillery group had their headquarters there.

Although of course altogether different, Lud was poor in contrast to Ben Shemen. Lud is, as you probably know, the ancient Lydda where Peter healed Aeneas (see Acts 9:32-35). A typical Palestinian town, its streets are narrow and indescribably filthy, the roads broken and uneven, and torturous. The houses were interesting, being high built, only dimly lighted and suggestive of mystery. I should judge that in the older parts, the scene is similar to that obtaining in Peter's day. Lud eventually became important as a Supply Base, and a few months after I saw it, came under the domination of our sanitary authorities, and huge encampments, and a big railway centre were made. The inhabitants were mostly Syrians, invariably abject looking, poor and dirty. A feature, very noticeable was the number of blind and partly blind folk. This is of course due to the frightful unsanitary conditions, and inadequate medical facilities. Writing from my knowledge of India, there is no doubt that in a comparatively short time, this disease will become almost stamped out as the result of medical missionary, and governmental enterprise.[188]

We had to pay a stiff price for our various purchases, matches for instance costing 2 piastres, 5d per box and poor ones at that.

---

188 See www.ncbi.nlm.nih.gov/pmc/articles/PMC2636602/ and jalili.co/covi/02_Histpreamb.htm concerning the fact that there is still a high percentage of preventable blindness in Palestine, in comparison with Israel and other parts of the Western world.

The day after our visit to Lud was enlivened for us by the attempts of Johnny to put our section out of action. His first shot hit the ridge just in front of us, and a succession of shells whistling over us, burst just beyond us. The nearest was less than 50 yds away. Strangely enough, he used only high explosive shells. If he had used shrapnel, someone would certainly have been hit, for he could then have "timed" them to burst overhead. As it was, the ridge in front just protected us from a direct hit. I found out subsequently that our bursts were far superior to the Turks'. Whenever one of our "pills" burst, the effect was uniformly broadcast, i.e. in all directions but the direction of Johnny's bursts were forward and upward only. If the shells which dropped near us had been as good as ours, there would have certainly been casualties. As it was, we all escaped scot free. There was the inevitable humorous side to the incident. This was created mainly by our dives for cover. A "funk" hole, dug at the side of our gun and calculated to hold about four men, afforded shelter at one time to nine. The fellow who was first in and got underneath felt ill and sore afterwards. One oncoming shell found five of us by the gun and we all promptly dived for cover in the gun trail in which there was room for two at a squeeze, but we all got in. The lad who lost a length of skin off his shin was a capital linguist. Our right section guns which were in position about ¾ mile away subsequently by counter battery fire, succeeded in drawing off the Turk's attention. Personally, I felt very loose inwardly, but I was graciously blessed with the assurance that whatever the issue, I was alright anyhow. Strangely enough perhaps, on this and similar occasions, I never felt led to ask God for protection of life and limb so much as for the grace to conduct myself in demeanour and action as becoming one whose trust was in Jesus Christ, and for the inward assurance that no matter what happened, I was safe for aye in His tender keeping, so that come life or come death, I was His. Except for one occasion when I was caught in a sudden panic about which I will write at the proper stage, I always experienced the answer to my prayers in the shape of a sense of his peace that passeth all understanding. To Him and to Him alone be all the glory. Toward evening, an aeroplane of ours came over to try and find the offending gun and apparently found it, but the observer bungled by not giving us his height and so we were unable to get the range. For several days this gun played havoc behind our lines and on one occasion, we watched the shelling of a supply column galloping across the plain near us. Two days afterwards, he shelled the mule lines of the South African Artillery, causing casualties and the following day shelled Ben Shamen as referred to previously. Several attempts were made to correctly locate this gun, but it was apparently well concealed and probably was what is known as a "runner", being concealed in a cave when not in action and run out for each "shoot." The man in charge was a bit of a sport, for on every occasion when we tried to get him, he would cease fire and lie low until we had ceased fire and then he would promptly open out again. It was not until several weeks after the above incidents occurred that he was eventually correctly observed by a South African Artillery officer, and our right section forthwith silenced him for good.

With regard to Johnny's knowledge of our position, it struck us as most remarkable that natives were allowed to pass to and fro near to our guns. There is hardly any doubt but that spies communicated our whereabouts.

While in this position I was again compelled to sample the medical arrangements, the wet ground being responsible for a sharp dose of lumbago. When I did eventually report sick it was as much as I could manage to walk about. The doctor came to the gun position, had a look at me, gave me a few aspirin tabloids and told me to "carry on"! Of course I got no better and could do no heavy work, hence the detachment suffered from a shortage of one man. The following day, I just protested I couldn't carry on, and so was transferred to the wagon lines, in the place of another man who took my place. The doctor was not available this day, so not having been excused duty, I had to do duty amongst the horses. It had been steadily raining for several hours and I had perforce to erect my "bivvy" in the rain and get what little rest I could on the wet ground and now sodden blankets. A day later, the above treatment was repeated.

I however managed to purchas[sic] an extra issue of rum, and succeeded to sweating the trouble out somewhat, and thanks be to God and a still decent constitution, I eventually got fit again. Nobody who went sick, however bad they were got anything else than "medicine and duty." Even the horses were better cared for, for any sick were dosed, dieted and struck off duty.

This incident marked a change in my living, for henceforth I was a driver, and for the rest of my service abroad, I was with the horses. Although the work was harder, often unpleasant, and very trying, I rather welcomed it, for I knew nothing of horses and felt that I could improve upon the opportunity to add to my few accomplishments. How I fared will be duly recorded.

During our stay in this position, we were frequently wrathfully disgusted with our officers who as usual made themselves as comfortable as possible, caring not a jot about the men. Rations were invariably short, but the officers always collared a big share of the same, and we frequently had the chagrin of seeing them partaking of foodstuffs that by rights ought to have been ours, we, either going short, or without altogether. It will I guess be asked "Had you no remedy?" Yes, as a battery we could have complained to the higher authorities, but nobody dared to do so. The docility of our crowd was a thing most wonderful.

The wagon lines were in an olive grove, a pretty spot, but as the result of our occupation, desperately muddy. Where the horses stood was over ankle deep in mud, and everyone was covered in filth. But, - and I want to emphasize as a testimony - I was, on the whole, contented, and never at any time did I want to go back to the guns. There was every good reason for preferring the guns, and the lads couldn't understand my preference. It was solely due to the grace God supplied.

I soon found that the wagon lines were not a restful retreat, and I well remember my first night there when teams were turning out at all hours taking up ammunition to the guns and fetching fresh supplies from a dump ten miles away. Camels were tethered near my abode and rattled the stones all night. Cats and dogs from the neighbouring villages added their quota to the cacophony which was completed with the noise of the guns and bursting bombs on the other side of the ridge. I was lousy like everybody else, and my body companions did their best to make the night a lively one for me. Against the notes from which these details are written, I have added "Cheerio"! and as I write this I grin to myself. A sense of humour is a useful gift. I once heard a fellow here, whose food was seasoned with muck, say, "When I came out here, I expected to fight for the Holy Land, but I'm d--- d if I expected to have to eat it." No wonder the foreigners don't understand us.

During the day 23rd December, the Turk got fed up with our persistent attentions, and retreated a few miles, this resulting in our having a "cushy" time for a few days. On this day, I was able to write and get away a few letters, the first for over three weeks.

Dec 24th was made hideous with rain. It poured down all day. Food was scanty and all smoking materials non-existent. We were glad at sunset to crawl into our "bivvies", get between the wet blankets and go to sleep. During the night, the heavens opened and about 2 a.m. I was awakened by a flood which had flowed into my bivvy and was inches deep around me as I lay. I dragged the bed out on to a heap of stones which stood above the water, and drawing the blankets, from one of which I had wrung the water, over me, lay there until daybreak, when I found that several had had a similar experience. Some blighter roared out "A Merry Xmas" Oh!!!

Xmas Day 1917:

Shall I ever forget it? Not while memory lasts. Quite apart from it being Xmas Day, it was the worst day I ever spent. While it only rained intermittently, water and mud was everywhere. Let me tell you what the menu was. An issue of 8oz of bread to last the day. Breakfast 2oz bacon, 1pt tea with a little rum added. Dinner :- 3oz Boiled meat, 1pt tea, 1 orange: Tea:- 1pt tea, a small piece of cheese, 1 dessert spoonful of jam. Nearly all of us had parcels which we knew had been posted to us, but which were still undelivered, in fact we got but very little mail for two months. As for the much boasted bounty of the authorities who as per oft published memorandums at home, undertook to supply the armies with ½ lb pudding per man etc. etc. etc. ad lib, nothing ever reached us. Furthermore, from subsequent inquiries I made, I know of no units in the fighting areas then who did get anything except what their officers had managed to purchas for them. But I did hear of great doings at the Base and in units behind the firing lines.

Some of our lads managed to purchas some wine and got drunk and really for a moment I envied them. But with a big effort, I managed to read my Bible and found a solace in prayer. I tried to shave, but the cold made it an almost impossible task. Thoughts of home, try as I might, would impinge upon my mind. I confess to a strong desire to have with me some of those home folk, the fireside militarists who talked so glibly of fighting the war to a finish. During the day I was led by a certain instance to meditate on the subject of cheerfulness and as a result may some day hold forth to some forbearing audience upon that subject. One of our drivers, notorious by reason of his powerful voice suddenly slit the atmosphere with a song, the burden of which was "All that I ask is, love"- At first I admired the man who could sing amid such conditions and under such circumstances. (He wasn't drunk). I felt too I could appropriate a lesson thereby. But less than two minutes afterwards he was lividly cursing all things in general and the war in particular in a way that did one good to hear. (I make anyone a present of that admission). Was his former effort a symptom of cheerfulness?

During the day I re-pitched my bivvy over a bed of large stones so arranged as to permit of my lying on it with some degree of comfort, and ensuring, that if again the water flooded around, it would not reach my bedding. On active service, one early developed a wider definition of the word "comfort" Oh!

But I was glad at the close of the day to coil down on my stony couch.[189]

Boxing Day, praise God was a fine day, and we were thus enabled to dry our wet clothes, blankets etc.

I early found that there was a distinct "tone" in the language of the horse lines. At first, hardened as I thought I was to the vitriolic filth alas prevalent in the army, I was staggered by the language of our drivers. But although of course I ever held such as inexcusable, there was a certain amount of provocation, for what with the mud and the exasperating idiosyncrasies of the horses, one had a stiff task to keep evenly tempered and to refrain from expletives. During my experience as a driver I had various charges each of which at times "had fits", and I am not consistently good tempered, and so I could quite understand the verbal accomplishments of our boys. Towards the end of the campaign, I was given charge of two mules, and if any of my readers ever feel or suspect that I am getting smugly proud of myself, unduly docile, or in any way in need of "gingering up", they need only even whisper the word "mules" to me. Of course, I cannot be responsible for subsequent eventualities. They must accept the risk. But joking apart, no one but they who have worked among horses under active service conditions can possibly realise what a trying experience that work is. I have at times felt mortified at my loss of temper almost to the point of utter despair after a tussle with my animals. Poor beasts, they frequently had to suffer for our shortcomings.

On the evening of Boxing Day, I "mounted" my first picquet. It may interest you to know what that duty often consisted of. Picquet, is really a guard over the horses during the night, and the duty of the picquet is to ensure that no horses get loose, or come to harm in any way, and in the event

---

189 The H.A.G. Digest reported that the Corps Commander had sent Christmas greetings to the troops, adding "you may well be proud of the part you have played in the recent operations." On Christmas Day it was noted that at least 8 inches of rain fell in 20 hours, and transport difficulties limited the animals to half rations. *H.A.G Digest 181st Heavy Battery,* The Royal Artillery Museum, Royal Arsenal, Woolwich, London, SE18 6ST.

of any falling sick, to secure attention for them. The quietness of the horses invariably depended on the amount of food they were getting, and when, as when we were in Judea, they got but little to eat, picquet was a lively job. Sometimes the rope to which a string of horses was tied, would be gnawed through, and the breakage would have to be repaired while sundry equine friends would try and drag the parts in all directions. Sometimes a horse would get loose and would give the picquet a long chase through the dark before its re-capture. Occasionally a horse would get one or two legs over the rope and so run the risk of galling itself. This has to be set free at imminent risk to the driver. If one laid down, it had to be noticed that in doing so it didn't get its head chain round its throat and so strangle itself. Colic was a frequent complaint with them, and that meant walking the patient around sometimes for hours. Happy indeed the picquet who did his turn of duty without having some rotten task to perform.

We at last shifted from this position on Dec 29th. This was my first "stint" as a driver, and riding was most certainly much preferable to walking. When we started off, we expected rather bad travelling, and true enough, we found the roads in an awful condition. The first part of our journey lay though Lud where we watered, and here the ground near the troughs was a foot deep in slush. Of course this meant wet legs for the rest of the day. After leaving Lud, we began to pass through orange land, and in passing through one lane bordered by orange gardens, the officer in charge of our section of the column considerately halted awhile and then walked ahead a little out of sight. My! But those oranges were good. We picked several more en route to our halt, in fact, as we were on desperately short rations, we filled ourselves with the most delicious oranges. I personally ate – well no! I'm really ashamed to say how many. It was rather pretty country through which we passed, and the sprouting crops provided a delightfully green outlook which was a change after the stony scenes in the hills. The villages through which we passed appeared fairly populous, but as usual, very dirty. Noticeable were the women, who invariably looked ugly and withered although in many cases, quite young. I should say that this is due to the fact that it is the women who do the bulk of the work, certainly the hardest. It was quite a common sight in Palestine to see men and women going along the roads, the women bearing the loads, the men without. I have frequently seen the man riding an ass and the woman walking with a heavy load on her head. Quite a funny incident I saw once when an indignant Tommy stopped a couple proceeding along their way and made the man take upon himself the burden his wife was carrying, in spite of the vehement expostulation of the husband. One wondered how long the new arrangement lasted, and what happened to the wife later. We halted for the night in a sandy field 2 miles short of Jaffa, just off the main Jaffa to Ramleh road.

We resumed our journey about 9 a.m. the following morning toward Jaffa, and at once realised that we were getting into a new sort of country. For instance, we passed several Europeans, mainly French, and various European Jews. It was a treat to see the women and girls dressed, some of them in their Sunday best. Approaching Jaffa, we passed some fine houses, and soon everyone was agog. After the comparatively barren hill sides we had left, it was a treat to see so many fine poplars, cedars, cypress and firs. The first street in Jaffa proper was a splendid double road divided along its length in the centre by gardens in which, oh! delight, I recognised flowers familiar at home such as nasturtiums, sweet williams, marigolds, acquilegias etc. A fair size band stand and four fountains added to the ornamental effect. The name of this street by the way was Djemal Pacha St, after the Turkish generalissimo of that name. He had the reputation of being a tyrant, and so not very long after the British occupation, a fresh name was given to this delightful garden road. Our route lay right through this side of the city, and we were delighted with the scene. We "chi-icked" the girls, hurled jokes and witticisms at all and sundry and generally behaved as though we were out on a picnic. Crowds of soldiers were everywhere. I will leave a description of Jaffa to a later page and just here confine my detail to our trek. A "Home-reminding" touch had been given by the ubiquitous and "fond-of-advertising" Scot to some of the streets, and in passing

I saw Leith Walk, Argyle St, Edinboro' Rd etc. As soon as we got clear of Jaffa, the "going" was awful and "slicks" were very frequent and eventually we came to a halt for a couple of hours east of Sarona,[190] a German Colony 2 miles north of Jaffa. The chief reason however for halting here was that the firing line was only a few miles ahead and so it was necessary for us to wait until nightfall if we would get in unobserved. Hereabout I realised that to be a driver one had to forget they had nerves. Although euphemistically called roads, they were little more than worn tracks. We had to cross a bridge only recently repaired after the Turk had blown it up. When later I saw what we had crossed in the dark, I nearly had a fit, for there was just room to get over and a slight deviation from the centre of the bridge would have resulted in 20ft drop into the river bed below. Ditches were negotiated at the full gallop, and really all one could do was to sit tight, grip hard with the knees and trust to the horse keeping their feet. The hard travelling had its effect on the horses who were quite beaten out, and it took hours to get the whole column over the remaining three miles to the appointed gun positions; the last gun being finally dragged in by a reinforced team of 48 horses!! We were now, according to a map I had, in Samaria, hopeful of faring better than we did in the hill country of Judea.[191]

---

190 This is now part of Tel Aviv.
191 H.A.G. Digest reported that the 181st needed to move to a new location at Yazur, and then sent 120 horses for fattening. *H.A.G Digest 181st Heavy Battery*, The Royal Artillery Museum, Royal Arsenal, Woolwich, London, SE18 6ST.

Part IV In Samaria

Early the following morning Dec 31st, we were able to take stock of our new pitch and were delighted with the prospect. The guns were placed in an orange grove, the horse and wagon lines in a sandy field and the bivvies of the drivers in a eucalyptus plantation with a huge orange grove next to it. My! But didn't we give those oranges "socks". Every driver had a pile in his bivvy, we fed the horses on them for they were very fond of them. And such oranges as would have fetched 2d to 3d each in pace time. Oh but my mouth waters as I write. As a comfortable and easy situation, this was by far the best we had during the whole of the campaign.

During the day after our arrival, we saw groups of Jewish colonists with their belongings wending their way back to Jaffa. The Turk drove as many of the Jews as he could gather before him as he retreated, and all in Jaffa who failed to hide themselves or in any way dodge Johnny, had to leave their homes. Many anticipated events and left before the British entered, and it was many of these that we saw returning, rather a motley crowd, with their goods packed on camels, donkeys, horses and in all sorts of carts. But one felt the pathos of it, especially as probably many of them had already suffered persecution and banishment in other lands, in fact many of them had the look of stolid resignation of those used to that sort of thing. But I'm afraid few of our lads felt any sympathy with them for we had practical proof that a Jew is a Jew anywhere, always on the quest to bleed the Gentile. Some came to our camp selling various articles and the prices charged were such as only a Jew or an Eastern would have the audacity ask. Bread was charged @ 8piastres, 1/8, for a loaf weighing about 2lbs, eggs, plentiful hereabout, 4d ea, almonds, 20 for 2½d, figs, 12 for 2½d etc. in the neighbouring village, 2 piastres, 5d was asked for a cup of tea, and trouble was frequently caused through the soldier not first of all enquiring the cost of refreshments and then after partaking of the same to be charged a fantastical price. And this from people who professed the greatest relief and delight in the British occupation and who certainly stand to benefit most by it. At least that's how our lads argued.

A disappointment was in store for those of us drivers who were expecting an easier and pleasanter time in our new position, for two days after our arrival, the majority of us had to pack up again, and start off on our horses to a horse rest camp, instituted for such horses as ours that needed a rest and a feeding up after their excessive labours and privations of the past few months. That our horses were in need of such treatment was early evidenced, for although most of them were travelling out of draught, it was hard work knocking them along. At every rest halt, most of them laid down, and before we got properly started two had to be left behind, too weak to get going. Our route lay over the road through Jaffa we had previously come, and by the time we got to our evening halt, we had lost four horses, one dying en route, three being left at a veterinary hospital in Jaffa.

This being New Years Day, I of course thought long and often of the future, and wondered if perchance this year 1918 would be the last year of the war. I'm afraid few of us were optimistic enough to believe it would, and our forebodings were rather aided by the weather, for it rained in torrents. However, just after last feed, and before turning in for the night, we received a cigarette issue, and so many of our evil prognostications became surrendered to the soothing kiss of "My Lady Nicotine." I fancy I can hear the comment of one or two of the lady readers, "poor puny creatures, men!" After all, I suppose most of us are just big babys[sic], accepting the pipe as the baby does the rattle.

We had to go back to our previous position in order to pick up the horses belonging to the other section and so we traversed again the ground we came over a few days previously. One rather amusing experience happened to me as I rode along. I and my horses were part of a wagon team which included a native driver of the A.S.C. attached to us who rode just in front of me. As we jogged along, I got to singing, and among other favourite hymns sang "And can it be," "Who fathoms the eternal thought" "No not one" etc.[192] My Arab team mate evidently caught the infection, for he too sang, and so we sang in unharmonious duet, he in Arabic and I in English.

I thus spent two more nights on my old stone couch, for although we were due to leave the day after our arrival, it was adjudged wisest to give our horses a day's rest. A welcome relief was afforded by the arrival of a long overdue mail, which although scanty was worth getting. During the wait, I also completed the reading of a special Scripture Gift Society New Testament which I had given to me at Shellal. My! But that had been a real treat.

Early on the morning of Jan 4th we set off again on our long day's march. Fortunately, the weather had turned fine, and except for the deplorable roads, we had a fairly pleasant journey up to sunset. We passed through Ben Shemem and Lud and came to Ramleh where we halted for dinner. I would have liked to have had a look through Ramleh, but never got the chance for like every other place, it was "out of bounds" to the mere, common, herd, the "uncommissioned" soldier. It appeared a fine place from outside its walls. The tomb of St George is shown there.

The fine weather continued until we got near to Yebneh[193] where we struck a huge swamp. There were only wheel tracks to guide us across the safer parts of this, and as it was now sunset, we all supposed that we should wait until next morning before attempting to cross, but we with our inferior intelligences reckoned without our superior officer who forthwith continued on his way. One of the four wagons got stuck after going a few yards, and it had to be unloaded and dragged out by manual labour, for the horses couldn't get a footing in the mud. You will readily guess our plight. We struggled on, through the village until we came to a stream.

---

192 See Reflection Chapter for a copy of these hymns.
193 Also called Yavneh, or Jabneel.

Now clearly there was a ford somewhere, but nobody knew where. It was dark. There was positively not the least need for hurry, and we might well have decided to halt there until daylight. But no, the officer followed a track and essayed to cross the stream on his horse and eventually discovered what he thought was a place sufficiently shallow for the wagons to cross, and ordered the first wagon to drive through. It got stuck well in the centre of the stream. Most of the men's kits were on that, and as it stood, it was impossible to get anything off it except by wading hip deep through about 20 yds of running water with a soft bed to walk upon. But the idiot, even then, still persisted in his purpose and essayed to get another wagon, my wagon, which contained the cooks gear and the rations, across higher up the stream. Just as we got about half way across, two of the horses fell into a hole and dragged two others down with them. Fortunately mine kept their feet. So not only was the wagon stuck fast, but the drivers had the job of wading into the water amongst the struggling horses and unfastening their harness and their assisting the horses to their feet. Of course, our gentlemanly officer cursed the men and then decided we could go no further until daylight. We had to get the cook's stuff off the wagon and wade through the water with it to the bank where a fire was built and tea was made. Here I ought to add a tribute to the oft abused cooks. From time to time, these men had to work under the greatest difficulties and discomfort, and it was really marvellous how at times they ever succeeded in boiling water not to mention cook anything. For instance, on this occasion, a fire of wet wood was made on ground sodden with rain. And yet I do not remember our ever having to do without a meal through their failure, although sometimes we had to wait for our food when the elements and circumstances fought against them. They nearly always worked harder and longer than the rest, and never were as comfortable as the others. Rare were the praises, many were the abuses showered on them. Judging by our men, I assert that of all men who have done their bit in this war, the cooks of the fighting units have done a big share.

It was about 9 p.m. when our "leader of men" gave the order to prepare for spending the night where we were. The ground was running wet and all our kits, as stated before, were on the first wagon stuck in the stream. A few did wade after their bedding, but most of us including myself decided to make the best of things as we were. So I pulled a corn sack on over my legs, buttoned my overcoat well around me, fixed a saddle for a pillow, and pulling a saddle blanket over my head and shoulders, slept soundly until daybreak, not being awakened even by the rain which came down again heavily during the night. Of course, I was rather damp when I awoke. Another of our horses died during the night. At daybreak, we were able to judge the character of the land by the number of carcases lying around. From where we stood, we counted eight horse carcases. After a deal of trouble and hard work, we managed to get across the stream after breakfast, but even then, the track was for over a mile and a half, almost entirely submerged, and could only be followed by going straight toward such parts of the road ahead as lay above the water.

However, we eventually reached the spot assigned to us, a heavy sanded part just right for horses. Sand to us drivers was always welcome, for that meant not only clean horse lines, and mud-less work, but as the rain soaks through the sand, we could always keep the water from flowing into our bivvies. But here again we were provided with another instance of the super intelligence of the "higher orders." The advantage the camp had was was that it was fairly near the main supply dumps and so we could get plenty of forage. But to water, we had to go about two miles to Yebneh across the swamp, a trying journey at any time for horses, but especially for our weak crocks. As a result, we lost two in the water, they having fallen and being too weak to make the necessary effort to rise again. Obviously the extra food they got did them no good, as we had to do the journey twice per day, it was too much for many of them. The first night after our arrival, no less than eight of the poor beasts were "down" with colic, two of them subsequently dying.

I have notes of several experiences which happened to me while here, but I must only detail two or three, although all of them are more or less remarkable. I and a party of others had one morning to go back to the help of one of the two horses mentioned above as having been lost in the swamp. Previous to wading through the waters, we partly stripped, and left boots, breeches, coats etc. on a bank. To get to where the horse lay, we had to wade for about ¾ mile through streams and through mud that threatened to hold us fast. It made one sick to see the gallant efforts of the horse to regain its feet, but owing to the slippery mud and its weakness failed each time. We after much trouble, managed to get a blanket under the beast, and get it to its feet, but it was too weak to stand. While we were struggling the heavens opened again and soon we were just heaps of wet rags. We stood supporting the horse for some time in the hope that it would sufficiently regain its strength to enable it to walk unaided, but it had passed the limit of recovery. And so, after well over and hours hard work, we pulled it on to a bit of rising ground and there shot it. When we got back to our clothes of course they were saturated. The officer "got the wind up" about us, and we were ordered to get between the blankets and heavily dosed with rum, other chaps bringing the remainder of our meals. Not one of us suffered any ill effects. Now I was always prone to colds, thin blooded as the result of the sojourn in India and had had slight attacks of rheumatics in England. And yet, except for two sharp attacks of lumbago, one of rheumatics and a few colds, I was unaffected by the frequent soakings I got. At Yebneh, at one period, I wore wet clothing for nearly a fortnight, and had damp blankets for longer than that. In changing dirty underwear, I have had to lie on the clean stuff in order to dry it sufficiently to put on. During the whole of the winter 1917-18, and through all the wet weather, I had only a pair of drill "shorts" to cover my legs, not even possessing drawers. Furthermore, my only jacket was a dull one. (I ought to state here that according to orders, I handed all my serge clothing in at Shellal before we started off on our fighting stunts; and I and others who joined the Battery when I did, were not indented[194] for, when serge clothing was requisitioned for the rest of the men.) Of course I suffered from the cold, and yet as I have said, had no serious sickness. Primarily, I feel certain, I owe this immunity under God to the many prayers ever ascending in my behalf. Other men, physically my superiors, have gone under the strain, while I have been spared. Kept by the power of God, sustained by His grace, guarded by His hand, enfolded in His love. The memory is both humiliating and reassuring. I feel desperately unworthy of such providence, and yet I am encouraged for the future.

"The Lord hath helped me hitherto,

The Lord will help me still,"

The worst experiences I think I had was when not only the body, but the mind became numb. Sometimes any effort such as reading, writing etc., was quite beyond me, and I have sat, cold to the bone, and incapable of lucid though. Then I felt just on a level with the wretched shivering beasts in our lines. Or I have grown quite tired of efforts to combat the elements, to tie or fasten my bivvy so that the wind and rain are kept out, and have sat knowing from the silence around that others are suffering similarly. It was then that even thoughts of God were absent. One just didn't think at all. A sudden order to turn out and repair some damage somewhere would come as a blessed relief, and then I have sometimes thought "He knows, He sees, He cares," only sometimes mark you. Oh! I've a terrible long way to travel to reach the Pauline[195] standard, to be able to say "I have learned in whatsoever state therein to be content."

---

194 Fitted.
195 As in, the Apostle Paul, Philippians 4:11.

Reflections from the Diary

"I shall never be more than a mere camouflaged civilian."

Most readers feel an element of disappointment at the abrupt cut off of the diary. Where did he go next? How did he feel about it? Will he mention Barbara the mule? However, in spite of the unanswered questions, the dairy has, to this point, given a vivid perspective on life as a soldier in Palestine during the First World War. In the space of a few months, he has shared more than enough for readers to learn much from his careful jottings.

In his preface, Philip said that he especially hoped that readers would learn something about how God had helped him, and in the process of presenting his thoughts, he has given a rare insight into the way in which faith can be lived, even in a war. While there are accounts of faith and spirituality from other soldiers of this time, many focus on Chaplains or Officers, or on the telling of miraculous stories. This diary is a rare voice of an ordinary soldier among the ranks, exploring his own faith and feelings,[196] with an authenticity

---

196 There are written accounts connecting faith to the experience of the First World War. For example, H. Salkeld, *The Vital Year* (Harpenden: Gospel Standard Trust Publications, 1996) which is a published account of a young Christian soldier, serving in the EEF in the final year of the war. The author later became a Strict Baptist pastor, and he used his personal experiences in WWI to illustrate a religious theme or point. Philip Bryant, in contrast, records his thoughts, feelings and observations, in order to testify to his experience. Michael Snape, *God and the British Soldier: Religion and the British Army in the First and Second World Wars* (London and New York: Routledge, 2005) is a helpful exploration of the religion

145

that comes from experience. For him, faith is much more than formality, routine or ritual. It is personal, and touches every aspect of his life and is therefore very evident in his diary. It can be difficult to find words to describe another person's spirituality, but at his invitation, this final chapter seeks to do that, examining what his claim to walk with God looked like in real life: not just as a civilian in peaceful times, but as a Christian in Khaki, a man of faith in uniform.

Spirituality is concerned with experience, rather than beliefs.[197] In his Preface, he says that his intention in writing the diary is to show his readers how God has helped him. Yet, the absence of miraculous escapes and near-misses which might have been expected, is soon overshadowed by a sense of closeness and comfort he finds through friendship with God. Readers of his diary will notice that Philip regularly speaks of his personal experience of God as someone who is very real, and near to him: not as a distant Being, but as "Friend" and "Presence". By constantly using this kind of language, he shows that his awareness of God is defined by a dynamic and consistent sense of closeness, even when he himself is feeling miserable or depressed. Some might say that this is a much more helpful experience of the supernatural than the miraculous accounts other soldiers were more inclined to focus on. [198]

Although he finds it natural to talk about his faith and devotion, it is clear that there is nothing especially denominational about it. While his personal Christian commitment was born among the American Baptist missionaries in India and Burma, and then lived out among the Methodists in Britain, his diary is full of Christian friends and padres, meetings or Sabbath services, from a wide range of Christian denominations. His encounters pay little attention to a particular label, but rather, seem to focus on whether that friendship or experience leads to a closer walk with God. He uses these criteria when deciding whether a Wesleyan padre, was "A.1."[199] or not, or when appreciating the "fine evangelical preaching" of a Church of England padre.[200]It was obviously liberating for him to look at things

and spirituality of soldiers at this time. See also personal accounts, recorded by the Bible Society online:
www.biblesociety.org.uk/about-bible-society/our-work/world-war-1

197 Michael Downey, *Understanding Christian Spirituality* (New Jersey: Paulist Press, 1997), p.8.
198 Michael Snape, *God and the British Soldier: Religion and the British Army in the First and Second World Wars* (London and New York: Routledge, 2005), pp.45-57.
199 Diary: November 7th describing the Wesleyan Padre Mr Kelley.
200 Nov 7th.

in this way, since he could find fellowship with Christians from a range of backgrounds and traditions, among whom were the Salvation Army pal he shared a bivouac with,[201] or the small group from a siege artillery draft, who had formed a branch of the Soldiers' Christian Association, and whose studies he joined saying, "we held one meeting under some trees, and a glorious time it was."[202] His comment about his Salvation Army friend summarises his outlook and conviction that regardless of background, there is something that connects all believers together:

> *"In civil life he is a farm labourer, but we had much in common, as all Christians have."[203]*

His encounters with church traditions beyond his own Evangelical background is also of special interest. He seems to have even surprised himself by his openness to them, and at times felt challenged by them. Travelling across France, he paid close attention to the Roman Catholic shrines and crosses and in Italy to the ornate decoration of church buildings. He admits to deploring the "system and belief"[204] behind these things, which would be an expected Evangelical perspective, yet he can't help himself acknowledging their beauty and value, even if only as "art treasures."[205] In Italy he seems to have felt that the artefacts of religion represented nothing more than the power and oppression of the Church, contrasting them with people living in poverty, and wondering "if there were not some truth in an assertion that a priest ridden people is a poor people."[206] Yet in France, he felt that there was something helpful and useful in them, noting that

> *"these marks of devotion, ... were probably placed in these positions out of love to God and of a desire for service toward the fellow countrymen of the donors. I felt too something of the irresistible appeal it must make to the devout Catholics, the sight of this magnificent image of the Lord with arms outstretched in entreaty to a world of suffering, sinful humanity."[207]*

---

201 Shellal.
202 Cimino.
203 Shellal.
204 August 22nd.
205 August 25th.
206 August 24th.
207 August 22nd.

The apparent tension between these two perspectives of revulsion and appreciation is in reality explained by his own personal experience of devotion. For him, the sight of a hillside cross is positive because it serves the purpose of directing his thoughts upward to God, and wryly admits to being "something of a ritualist."[208] He can see how these things can help people in their devotion, and he shows appreciation for the heritage of Christian writers from these traditions, whose spirituality had been passed on in books he himself had read and benefited from. Yet there is no inconsistency for him to feel disgusted at other times by the presence of shrines, or the display of crucifixes and implements of the crucifixion he observed outside many churches.[209] In this context, they convey to him a barrier to God. He feels that they are nothing more than "crude 'aids',"that, "obscure the real Object of all true 'worship'."[210] He uses strong language on these occasions because he feels that such items become a religious object that "befogs the simple path of approach to God."[211] Even so, he still concludes, "Lord, make me very tolerant, very charitable,"[212] a sentiment which may not have been echoed by all of his intended readers.

His love of nature and his avid fascination with the world around him is another aspect of his spiritual perspective. In the first chapters of his diary, it is clear he has gone to the trouble of getting a map in order to study the journey and places he expects to visit. He relishes the opportunity to learn or see something new and is always on the look-out for something "of interest." In writing it down, it is clear that his main purpose is to help his readers know what it was like to be there, but more often than not, his real delight seems to be that the things he sees communicate something of God to him. He feels, as he looks around him, captivated by the magnificent natural beauty of the sights he sees on the way, that he is looking at a "Master Hand",[213]God's handiwork, and this encourages him to enjoy and delight in as much of it as he can. However, it would be unfair to just call him a lover of nature, or even an admirer of its Maker. For Philip, it is much deeper. Readers will have noticed that when he makes these observations, he talks about the way in which nature makes him actually feel closer to God. For Philip, the beauty and majesty of

208 August 23rd.
209 Cimino.
210 August 23rd.
211 August 23rd.
212 August 23rd.
213 August 22nd.

creation reveal the work of an unseen Creator to whom he feels close and connected to. Nature therefore become the means by which he deepens his appreciation of his "Friend." When he sees the sights of natural beauty he looks with wonder at God's wisdom and design, or is left feeling awestruck at its beauty, and yet it produces a feeling of God's all-embracing care and concern for him. Perhaps the best example of this is found in his account of a stunning view of the Alps, and his thoughts turn to a Bible passage familiar to him:

> *"These high flung peaks remind me of their Creator Who is my God and Father. To me, they represented in some measure the strength of Him Whose eye turneth to and fro throughout the whole earth, to show Himself strong on my behalf. The hand that shaped the Alps, guards me and mine."*[214]

Even human structures and great achievements in engineering construction remind him of his friendship with God. When passing through France, he noticed the honeycombed pattern of dwellings built into the cliff side, saying, "one huge rock with a dwelling hewed into it was very suggestive of 'The Rock of Ages' and I had a new conception of the Rock as a defence, a dwelling-place and an object of beauty."[215] A cleverly constructed bridge or the quirky design of a collection of dwellings are, in his opinion, the result of God-given ingenuity, even if they are merely a pale contrast to God's own creative work.[216] For him, nature is not just to be enjoyed, but appreciated, by recognising its "real value."[217] He is clearly grateful that he can look at the world in this way, noting that for him,

> *"the dominant idea running as a theme amid the others, is that of adoration to God for the marvellous work and beauty of His hands, for eyes to see them, and for senses to "taste" them, for that best expresses how the sights appealed to me."*[218]

Just as the admiration of grand scenery stirs a sense of devotion in him, so also small things lead him to a sense of thankfulness at God's provision of them. This can be seen in the way in which he writes

---

214 August 24th. The Bible passage he quotes is from 2 Chronicles 6:9.
215 August 21st.
216 August 23rd.
217 August 20th.
218 August 22nd.

about things he might normally have taken for granted – a swim in the sea in the midst of a stifling journey, an extra ration, a letter from home or making a Christian friend. His takes clear delight in admiring a scene or eating a fresh orange (especially if bought at a good price!) or appreciating a pretty face. To Philip, they are all blessings or gifts from his Master and Friend and they lead to a real sense of thankfulness within him. He even risks the disapproval of some of his readers, by giving thanks for decent tobacco to smoke,[219] and the rum ration in the cold and wet. Although he chides himself for not being as content as he thinks he ought to be, he displays a challenging and remarkable sense of gratitude, and appreciation in such difficult circumstances. It is no better seen than the occasion, with nowhere comfortable to sleep, when he simply records "I turned into 'bed' on boards with a feeling that I had again had a wonderful day!"[220]

The theme that runs through all these experiences for him, whether discussing nature, or its gifts, is that they invariably make him feel that God is near and has a personal concern for him. He feels that God is his Creator and Provider. This sense of personal friendship with God is for Philip the ultimate meaning of his life. It is cultivated and sustained though his devotional pattern of daily prayer, Bible-reading and hymn-singing. From his earliest Christian experiences in India, these regular daily habits would have been developed. American Baptists and British Methodists alike would have taught that they were necessary for a healthy spiritual life. It is noticeable, however, that there is no hint of pious duty in the descriptions of his devotional patterns. He actively seeks them out, and revels in the opportunity to find a quiet place for intimate and personal communion with God. He did not feel the need to be in a chapel or holy place to sustain this either. He believed he met with God wherever he could find a quiet place with his Bible and prayer, whether on the footboard of the train, in the misery of a rain-soaked bed, or even in the "toilette!"[221] Even though he found Bible-reading a struggle at times, he describes it as taking a "tonic,"[222] and speaks of his devotions in a personal and non-religious way. To Philip it is

219 Smoking, of course, was not perceived as such a health risk as in modern times. Serious medical research took place from the early 20th Century, but smoking was increasingly thought of as a vice by Evangelicals, along with drinking alcohol. In 1874, the popular evangelical preacher, C.H. Spurgeon stirred up a debate in his statement that he would "smoke to the glory of God". Some of the discussion is documented here: www.spurgeon.org/misc/cigars.htm.
220 August 22nd.
221 August 21st where he also notes he spent half an hour of quiet time with God.
222 October 15th.

simply a talk with "The Friend,"[223] and the places in which he meets with Him he calls a "Bethel"[224] – even if their location is unusual:

> *"as an instance of strange 'Bethels,' I record that I sat on the footboard in the rear of the car and had a very fine and helpful time with God. The rattle of the car drowned my somewhat subdued singing."*[225]

It is noticeable that the regular outcome of his devotional times is a sense of knowing "The Presence," and of being reminded of God's care. He often describes a real feeling of joy and a calm sense of trust and peace that result from them. For example, he notes on one occasion that

> *"No provision for a service had been made so I got aside and had a good read, prayer & meditation. A rumour got abroad that a German submarine was sunk outside the harbour during the night. I cannot vouch for the truth of it, but the rumour was productive in me of a sense of reassurance that I am in the safe keeping of Him who has my name engraved on the palm of His hand."*[226]

Although Bible-reading was a means of guidance and direction for him, it is clear that its main role in Philip's life is that he actually feels closer to God through it. It is unsurprising, therefore, that the Bible is so precious to him. It is not a text book, or rule book, or even a lucky charm,[227] but a lifeline to his Friend, a source of great comfort in difficult times, and the reassurance of his Master's voice speaking. It explains, too, why memorising and recalling passages of Scripture was also important to him, and is one of the reasons he was able to cope with his war time experiences. A clear example of this is

---

223 August 23rd, Oct 5th, Nov 7th.
224 August 28th and see footnote. Alluding to Genesis 28:16-18.
225 August 27th. ·
226 August 19th.
227 Many soldiers used to cope with the fear of danger by using mascots and lucky charms. The small pocket Bible, carried by many soldiers was often treated as a lucky thing to have. Stories circulated about Bibles that had "taken a bullet," saving those who carried them. Unfortunately, there were also stories of Bibles which bullets passed right through as well. See Michael Snape, *God and the British Soldier: Religion and the British Army in the First and Second World Wars* (London and New York: Routledge, 2005), p33-38.

illustrated in his special mention of Psalm 121.[228] He felt this passage was a special text to which God had directly drawn his attention. He was at the front line, in range of enemy artillery, exhausted and anxious. He was about to snatch a few hours sleep before the next day's hostile operations, yet he comments,

> *"as you will understand, I thought hard over the possibilities of the day ahead, but Psalm 121 recurred to my mind and I felt quite assured and easy in mind and spirit."[229]*

Obviously, he does not deny his fears, but reading and thinking about the verses of Scripture enabled him to find a source of help and strength beyond his own anxiety and resources. This kind of experience is something that many might still envy or aspire to today.

On one occasion, he described the inclusion of hymn-singing in his devotional time. It might have been "subdued," on the footboard of the train, but singing hymns was also a pivotal part of his personal devotional life. Methodists were well known for their love of hymnody,[230] and Philip's diary often includes quotes from hymns, as well as a record of times when he sang them. One of the most vivid examples of Philip's love of hymns, and their usefulness and comfort to him, is recorded in the truck journey he took with a local Arab driver. He began singing some of his "favourites," as he called them, and was delighted that the driver joined in with them, albeit making up his own words in Arabic! Philip named three hymns, the words of which clearly had heartfelt meaning for him, and presumably, he hoped, for his readers since he expected them to recognise the hymns just by quoting their titles. Since the three hymns might be less

---

228 Oct 15th and Oct 26th. "...my help cometh from the Lord, which made heaven and earth..." Psalm 121 (AV).

229 October 26th.

230 "Sing lustily and with good courage. Beware of singing as if you were half dead, or half asleep; but lift up your voice with strength," John Wesley, "Directions for Singing, A Collection of Hymns for the Use of the People Called Methodists," cited in Franz Hildebrandt, and Oliver A. Beckerlegge, (Eds), *The Works of John Wesley Vol. 7* (Oxford: Clarendon Press, 1983), p765. John Henry Bett, the Methodist minister who married Philip and Millie at Grove Chapel, had a special interest in Wesleyan hymnody, having recently published *The Hymns of Methodism* (London: Paternoster, 1913). He later wrote the preface to Manning, Bernard L., *The Hymns of Wesley and Watts: Five Papers* (London: Epworth Press, 1942) and Bett also published *The Spirit of Methodism* (London: Epworth, 1938) and *What Methodists Believe and Preach.* (London: Epworth press, 1938).

familiar to readers a Century later, it is worth examining them briefly. They contain a broad and helpful summary of the heart of his faith and of the way in which he applied it to his life. The first hymn he refers to is "And Can it be?"[231] This well-known Methodist Hymn focuses on the amazement and wonder of enjoying and experiencing God's salvation in Jesus:

> *And can it be that I should gain*
> *An interest in the Saviour's blood?*
> *Died He for me, who caused His pain—*
> *For me, who Him to death pursued?*
> *Amazing love! How can it be,*
> *That Thou, my God, shouldst die for me?*
>
> *He left His Father's throne above*
> *So free, so infinite His grace—*
> *Emptied Himself of all but love,*
> *And bled for Adam's helpless race:*
> *'Tis mercy all, immense and free,*
> *For O my God, it found out me!*
>
> *Long my imprisoned spirit lay,*
> *Fast bound in sin and nature's night;*
> *Thine eye diffused a quickening ray—*
> *I woke, the dungeon flamed with light;*
> *My chains fell off, my heart was free,*
> *I rose, went forth, and followed Thee.*
>
> *No condemnation now I dread;*
> *Jesus, and all in Him, is mine;*
> *Alive in Him, my living Head,*
> *And clothed in righteousness divine,*
> *Bold I approach th'eternal throne,*
> *And claim the crown, through Christ my own.*

Perhaps his readers could imagine him singing these words as he bumped along a desert track, rejoicing in his chains falling off and his heart being set free! The second title he gives is "Who Fathoms the Eternal Thought."[232] It is easy to see how the words of this hymn could

---

231 Charles Wesley (1707-1788).
232 Written by John Greeleaf Whittier (1807-1892), an American Quaker and anti-slavery campaigner, better known as the author of the hymn "Dear Lord and Father of Mankind."

have been very meaningful to a soldier in active service. Its theme is finding trust in God when life seems puzzling or when difficult things happen. The following verses in particular highlight these thoughts:

> *1. Who fathoms the eternal thought?*
> *Who talks of scheme and plan?*
> *The Lord is God! He needeth not*
> *The poor device of man.*

> *3. Here in the maddening maze of things,*
> *When tossed by storm and flood,*
> *To one fixed ground my spirit clings;*
> *I know that God is good!*

> *9. I know not where His islands lift*
> *Their fronded palms in air;*
> *I only know I cannot drift*
> *Beyond His love and care.*

A real test of faith is to find God's goodness in trials, and Philip enjoyed this hymn as a favourite, and as a simple reminder that nothing could cause him to drift beyond God's love and care. The third hymn he mentioned on this occasion is "No Not One."[233] This hymn uses simple verses and repetition, popular at the time, to convey a simple and real sense of the unique kind of friendship a believer has with Jesus. Perhaps, more than all the others, the words of this one seem to summarise the very essence of the faith Philip portrays in his diary. He really seems to show, as the words say, that there isn't an hour in which friendship with Jesus is not apparent or helpful to him:

> *1. There's not a Friend like the lowly Jesus:*
> *No, not one! No, not one!*
> *None else could heal all our souls' diseases:*
> *No, not one! No, not one!*

> *(Refrain)*
> *Jesus knows all about our struggles;*
> *He will guide 'til the day is done:*
> *There's not a Friend like the lowly Jesus:*
> *No, not one! No, not one!*

---

233 Written by Johnson Oatman Jr (1856 – 1922), an American Methodist hymn writer and businessman.

2. There's not an hour that He is not near us,
No, not one! No, not one!
No night so dark, but His love can cheer us,
No, not one! No, not one!

3. Did ever saint find this Friend forsake him?
No, not one! No, not one!
Or sinner find that He would not take him?
No, not one! No, not one!

4. Was e'er a gift like the Saviour given?
No, not one! No, not one!
Will He refuse us the bliss of heaven?
No, not one! No, not one!

For Philip, devotional hymn-singing, prayerfulness, and Bible-reading, are his direct line to Jesus. His methods are simple, but the results are deep. An important fourth dimension to his spiritual life is his sense of connection with other believers. His personal times of reflection do not conceal a merely private faith. There is a definite communal dimension to it. For example, he tells his readers how he misses the Christian companionship of his family, and friends in his home churches. He liked to think of himself praying together with them at the same time, even though separated by geography. On one occasion he put it like this:

> *"Naturally I felt very wistful about 6 p.m. and longed to slide into the pew at Groves or Haxby. Ah well, I could still help in those services, and I believe I did. Prayer has a wonderful reach and influence."*[234]

He also values the Christian friends he makes through the course of the campaign, attends services of worship, and seeks gatherings for prayer as well as other special Christian meetings to find fellowship. Regarding Church services, he appears to have been instrumental in encouraging them to take place, particularly at the base in Cimino, and was an enthusiastic supporter of the padre there.[235] It was so important to him that if his usual Sunday pattern of meeting with

---

234 October 6th.
235 Cimino.

others for worship was not possible, it affected him, as he said on one occasion,

> *"it was hard to realise it was Sunday, and I felt out of tune all day, but a good read of my Sword helped me to sense the Presence."*[236]

He seems to have especially valued the opportunities to meet with other Christians at the Soldiers Homes.[237] One of the attractions would undoubtedly have been the facilities, and little luxuries they offered, but he obviously enjoyed the meetings held there, and becomes fond enough of the people who ran them to mention their names. The knowledge that such people are praying for him is a great source of strength and comfort to him, as he recalls on one occasion:

> *"During the evening I got a little "blueish" and thought wistfully of home, and the Soldier's Welcome at Winchester where I knew I was prayed for. It gives one tremendous confidence when they know that such a power of prayer is exercised by so many on his behalf."*[238]

His faith gave him a real sense of connection and belonging to a wider family, and was an additional source of help and encouragement to him.

In addition to his feeling of God's presence and care, made known through nature and his devotional life, Philip also exhibits a strong sense of calling and purpose in his experience as a soldier. Fighting in Palestine and the historic Bible-lands made many soldiers feel like this, even those with a nominal faith. One of the effects of being in the region is that it brings Philip's Bible knowledge alive, and makes his understating more vivid. It gives him a feeling of heritage and reminds him of a faith that is rooted in history. On one occasion, at El Kantara, he observes

> *"One and one only well worn track could be distinguished, and that was the oldest highway in the world along which the travellers long before the time of Abraham and Abraham himself passed. In fact, all*

---

236 August 26th.
237 See footnote, August 18th.
238 August 19th.

> *the scripturally recorded journeys from Palestine to Egypt took place along this road."*[239]

Another time, stopping between Beersheba and Karm, he made similar observations,

> *"we halted at a huge well, one existent in patriarchal days and probably used by the wandering Israelites."*[240]

Even the constant annoyance of flies seemed to draw him to Biblical themes, suggesting wryly that "the plague of flies has only been partially suspended!"[241] These experiences obviously made him feel as if he was walking in the footsteps of a family of faith who had gone before him. He wondered if he'd ever see Jerusalem, "the Holy City,"[242] as he calls it, and recorded, when reaching the western Judean hills, that he "felt conscious of being on historic ground."[243]

Many soldiers serving in the region shared Philip's sense of a higher calling and purpose in their campaigns.[244] In general, British soldiers held deep moral convictions about the cause they were fighting for, partly because they considered the initial actions of the Central Powers to have been unlawful, and partly because it was felt that the enemy used immoral methods of warfare.[245] The strong sense of moral purpose also meant that soldiers could easily become indignant towards allies who seemed more ambivalent about the war,[246] and was one of the factors that made them feel resentful when their own officers exhibited selfishness, cruelty or ignorance. With other soldiers, Philip laments the enemy's dubious methods and the selfish actions and attitudes of some of their own officers.[247] He was critical of the times when there was a lack of care and services for

---

239 October 15th.

240 November 2nd.

241 Part II On the Desert, and footnote. See also Shellal.

242 August 28th.

243 Part III In Judea.

244 Michael Snape, *God and the British Soldier: Religion and the British Army in the First and Second World Wars* (London and New York: Routledge, 2005), chapter 5, Religion, morality and war, p187ff.

245 Especially the apparent lack of distinction made between civilian and military.

246 "...some English speaking Italian soldiers frankly told some of our lads that they didn't care for their job, and but for England, the war would have been over and they would be back in their homes. Of course, the Italians were soon in disfavour with our troops..." August 24th.

247 August 27th Cimino, 26th October etc.

troops.[248] In addition to these factors, military service in the Middle East gave soldiers the added dimension of feeling that Palestine was in wrong hands.

Philip reveals, albeit in a humorous anecdote, the widespread feeling among the ranks that there was a higher purpose in the Palestine campaign, relating on one occasion

> *"I once heard a fellow here, whose food was seasoned with muck, say, 'When I came out here, I expected to fight for the Holy Land, but I'm d--- d if I'm expected to have to eat it.'"[249]*

For Philip, there was definitely a spiritual dimension to war in the Holy Land, and with it, a real feeling of a higher, or even holy calling. For him, there are lands worth defending and fighting for, not least, the region of Holy Land in which he served. He had noticed that the French had a particular attachment to their homeland. In a touching observation, he empathises with the way in which they seem so devoted to their country, saying

> *"We felt that we understood in part at least the wonderful "land love" of the French."[250]*

For Philip, there is a special interest in the land in which he was fighting. His strong sense of purpose and calling in this respect, is clarified for him at a meeting he attended at Lord Kitchener's Soldiers' Home near Mustapha Pasha. Miss Mitchell, the speaker on this occasion, spoke about various Bible prophecies relating to God's purposes for the land of Israel:

> *"She told her huge audience that they were in the truest sense of the word, crusaders, instruments of God for the working out of His wonderful purposes. She told of the doubtful character of the old crusaders, and pleaded that the new crusaders as God's chosen men give their lives to Him, to live for Him, and if it be His will, to die for Him. The interest of the hearers was intense, and few if any left the hall without a new ideal, and a strengthened purpose...From that day to*

---

248 e.g. Xmas Day 1917.
249 End of entry December 15th.
250 August 23rd.

this, I have never lost the sense of God's possession, and "fed up" as I have been often, I have ever remembered my high calling."[251]

It seems that there is a real attraction for in him in thinking of himself as a "new crusader," especially in a reinvented form, agreeing with Miss Mitchell's description of the doubtful character of the old Crusaders of the Middle Ages. He also thought this concept could have inspired more troops if padres had emphasised it better.[252] It was not that such ideals made war seem more glamorous to him. It definitely didn't. He makes no secret of his own awareness of its horrors, and he readily questions whether there might have been better ways to accomplish its aims. He certainly feels that there were those, more distant from real fighting, who almost relished the idea of war far too easily, because they had never contemplated or experienced its hell.[253] However, he still feels, albeit reluctantly, that his particular campaign was part of a holy war,[254] and that the idea of being a new crusader provided a framework he could use to make sense of what he was doing there. It helped him see himself, and his fellow servicemen, as part of a higher purpose and calling, serving a cause under the watchful guidance of his Heavenly Master. Once again, even here, the concluding theme in Philip's thoughts is his sense of friendship with God.

However, the most practical expression of his faith is seen in his ability to cope with, and make sense of, suffering, bereavement and the possibility of death. If his intention was for his readers to see how God had helped him, this is surely the ultimate test. British Soldiers were encouraged, through official channels, especially the ministry of chaplains, to prepare for death by entrusting themselves to God's care and forgiveness. "A Soldier's Prayer," for example, was distributed on small cards in the First World War for each serviceman to keep in his cap. It focuses on the need for forgiveness, peace, power and blessing:

*"Almighty and most merciful Father,
Forgive me my sins,*

---

251 Part II On the Desert.
252 Part II On the Desert. Woodward notes that some chaplains did do this, and inspired men , many of whom shared the feeling of a religious significance to their campaign: David Woodward, *Forgotten Soldiers of the First World War* (Stroud: Tempus, 2007), pp192-195.
253 November 7th.
254 November 7th.

> *Grant me Thy peace,*
> *Give me Thy power,*
> *Bless me in life and death for Jesus Christ's sake. Amen."*[255]

There is, however, an enriching depth to Philip's perspective that is much more developed than this. Philip's experience of God leads him to an insight and confidence that some may find surprising, since he claims that his friendship with God frees him from an ultimate interest in his own personal safety. In one of the prayers he records, he puts it this way:

> *"on this and similar occasions, I never felt led to ask God for protection of life and limb so much as for the grace to conduct myself in demeanour and action as becoming one whose trust was in Jesus Christ, and for the inward assurance that no matter what happened, I was safe for aye in His tender keeping, so that come life or come death, I was His. "*[256]

This profound perspective states that safety, even in war, simply meant being with God. It reveals that Philip had a deep assurance that beyond death, this Friendship must continue. This is not an isolated idea. He mentions the personal benefits drawn from his ability to talk to God and trust Him in the experience of suffering and fear, saying again, on one occasion,

> *"I always experienced the answer to my prayers in the shape of a sense of his peace that passeth all understanding."*[257]

Philip believes that God answered his prayers, not necessarily in the form of outward physical protection, but by giving him inner peace. This did not mean he wasn't scared. He's quite open about the reality of feeling afraid, and admits to experiencing at least one panic-attack, which, it seems, he intended to elaborate on more fully in the lost volume. Nor does he hide the realities of his nervous breakdown in previous years. However, his talks with "the Friend" seem to turn his fears to trust and peace. Somehow or other, he feels that from the beginning to the end of his journey, he is being guided, and cared for in life even if possible injury or death await him.

---

255 A Soldier's Prayer, IWM 41. 22/3-8.
256 December 15th.
257 December 15th.

Many soldiers thought that there was a "bullet with their name on it," a rather impersonal and fatalistic idea originating in WWI that when your time is up, it's up.[258] Philip's experience is different. His words convey the idea that he felt as if there was a personal God in control of his events and circumstances. Some might call this a belief in providence, and Philip uses that term,[259] but for him it was not a theoretical concept, but a practical reality, as he concludes towards the end of the diary,

> "...and then I have sometimes thought 'He knows, He sees, He cares.'"[260]

Perhaps Philip did think that there could be a "bullet with his name on," or a time when his "number might be up," but his real attention was on the feeling that God would be close to him, to intervene in a special or personal way, offering guidance and protection in a dangerous situation, or to help him face injury or death itself with confidence and strength. Whichever outcome, the focus on God's personal care for him helped him to be both courageous and content, even though he felt he still had a long way to go to feel it all the time.[261]

Philip's experience of God also helped him cope with actual sadness and bereavement. While in active service, he receives news of his father's death at home and that of a close friend killed in action. In both cases, his loss is tinged with the hope, or belief, that they shared in eternal life. Concerning his father he writes,

> "here I couldn't feel sad even if I wanted to, for Dad knew God as his Father and Friend, and to him, death was a glorious release from a life the latter part of which was one of the acutest kind of suffering. Nay, I rejoiced over the Christian hope, that they in Christ who pass away, pass straight into the presence of the King,"[262]

---

258 The idea being that when your time is up, it's just up. Michael Snape, *God and the British Soldier: Religion and the British Army in the First and Second World Wars* (London and New York: Routledge, 2005), p.28ff., observes that this particular view didn't appear to have made men braver, or cause them to rush headlong when going over the top in trench warfare.

259 Part IV In Samaria.

260 Part IV In Samaria.

261 November 7th Part IV In Samaria.

262 November 7th.

He felt badly hit by news of the death of his friend Harry Jackson in France, but was comforted by the thought of their shared Christian faith, writing that

> *"it was a keen satisfaction to remember that Harry was known of his Lord and Master, and that his death in action was the entry into the longer life where his talent will have full play and scope. Young as he was, he was old in his experience of the saving and keeping grace of God, and the sense of loss was tempered by the knowledge that he is now with the King whom he loved and served so well."*[263]

By focusing on their mutual hope of eternal life, he was enabled to cope with the sadness and the reality of earthly separation. When reflecting on his father's death the loss is bridged by a sense of closeness, even though he had died, and their shared faith kept him personally conscious of his own certainty of seeing them again:

> *"Certainly, Dad seems nearer now than ever before, and Heaven itself as the homeland of which earth is but as a colony, or as halting place en route."*[264]

Finding refuge in God, in the context of war, and death, provided a deeper well to draw from than just a British "stiff upper lip", or the Tommy's cheerfulness, especially as he found the characteristic of cheerfulness a personal challenge.[265] The certainty of knowing Jesus as his constant Friend, was the lens through which he saw the whole of life. Beauty caused him to offer up thanks to Him, sadness made him find comfort in Him, and suffering drove him straight to God as the ultimate source of courage.

A number of aspects of Philip's faith and spirituality have been touched on in this chapter. They have highlighted a maturity of faith that was tried and tested in such a way that there is a ring of authenticity and even authority in his experiences. The pages of his diary describe someone who seems to know what it is like to live *with*, and live *in* Christ each day, whether in peacetime or at war. Philip is

---

263 Part III In Judea (Dec 4th).
264 November 7th.
265 "...they met the situation by singing songs. The spirits of some is a thing beyond comprehension, but appears to be a striking characteristic of the British Tommy who will sing & joke amid the most depressing conditions and circumstances." August 18th. See also Nov 2nd and Part IV In Samaria.

an example of what many generations before and after him have simply described as "abiding in Christ."[266] Philip does not hide his flaws: the fact that he got angry, frightened, depressed and anxious. Nor does he hide the fact that he witnessed harrowing things. But whatever happens around him, he ends up returning to a place of living, or abiding, in the One he calls his Friend, and Master. Many have found that it is often in a challenge or crisis that they have really understood what walking with God is meant to be like, and in some ways this is true for Philip Bryant. He acknowledges on one occasion that

> *"Only those who have ever been denied the usual means of grace, the quiet room, the hushed stillness, the help of books etc. can sympathise with my difficulties. And yet, rarely in ordinary life have I enjoyed such an overwhelming sense of the Master's nearness. He revealed Himself so fully, that I got into the habit of conversational talks with Him."[267]*

A decade earlier he preached his "first sermon,"[268] on the theme of walking with God. He was inviting his hearers to think about what it might look like if God lived in them, and if they walked with Him. He wrote

> *"most of us are more or less conversant with the thought of God dwelling in us...Whatever God is, is to come out in my life. Oh what a humbling theme we have....Supposing that God walks about in me, what sort of life shall I lead? Of course if God is love, and God is going to walk in me, I must walk in love and love is to be the atmosphere that surrounds me on every side...God is light and therefore if God walks in me my path must be a bright one..."[269]*

His diary certainly seems to be a living illustration of these truths. At the very least, Philip Bryant was trying to put into practice the ideas he preached. In 1906, he considered it a "humbling theme," but over the years, walking with God had come to define his life, not just

---

266 John 15:4 where Jesus says to His followers "Abide in me" or in more modern translations "Remain in me."
267 Cimino, following August 28th.
268 Appendix I.
269 Ibid.

his sermon. His overwhelming conviction was not that life should be perfect, or trouble free, but that its true meaning was found in a deep, practical and personal friendship with Jesus Christ. Philip Bryant's final words, "Lord, I come!" are an indication, that even in old age, he continued to think of death, as well as life, as an ongoing walk with God. John Wesley is famously once said to have remarked,

> *"Our people die well! The world may find fault with our opinions, but the world cannot deny that our people die well."*[270]

Philip knew the secret of dying well, because he knew the secret of living well. He may have been a "camouflaged civilian," but beneath the uniform there was more than a civilian: there was a man "full of faith and devotion,"[271] who, even in the experience of war could say with conviction,

> *"and so we live together,*
>
> *my Friend and I."*[272]

---

270 The famous statement, made by John Wesley to a doctor, related in Luke Wiseman, *Charles Wesley: Evangelist and Poet,* (London: Epworth, 1932). Also quoted in Joseph D. McPherson, *"Our People Die Well": Glorious Accounts of Early Methodists at Death's Door,* (Bloomington, IN: AuthorHouse, 2008), p.xxv.
271 Appendix II.
272 August 23rd.

Appendix I

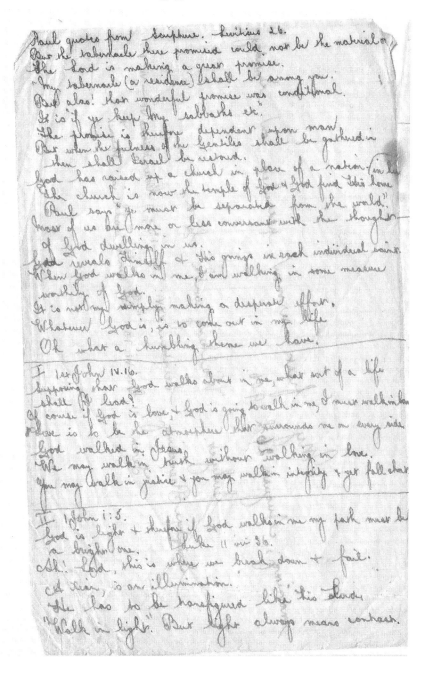

Paul quotes from Scripture. Leviticus 26.
But the tabernacle here promised could not be the material or
The Lord is making a great promise.
"My tabernacle (or residence) shall be among you."
But also! that wonderful promise was conditional.
It is "if ye keep my sabbaths etc."
The promise is therefore dependent upon man.
But when the fulness of the Gentiles shall be gathered in
then shall Israel be restored.
God has raised up a church in place of a nation. (in the
The church is now the temple of God & God find this home.
Paul say "ye must be separated from the world".
Most of us are more or less conversant with the thought
of God dwelling in us.
God reveals Himself & His grace in each individual saint.
When God walks in me, I am walking in some measure
worthy of God.
It is not my simply making a desperate effort.
Whatever God is, is to come out in my life.
Oh what a humbling theme we have.

I 1st John IV. 16.
Supposing that God walks about in me, what sort of a life
shall I lead?
Of course if God is love, & God's going to walk in me, I must walk in love
Love is to be the atmosphere that surrounds me on every side
God walked in Jesus.
We may walk in truth without walking in love.
You may walk in justice & you may walk in integrity & yet fall short

II 1 John 1:5.
God is light & therefore if God walks in me my path must be
a bright one.   Luke 11 vv 36.
Ah! God, this is where we break down & fail.
A risen, is our illumination.
We has to be transfigured like this study.
"Walk in light". But light always means contrast.

My first sermon; preached on Sunday morning, August 26th 1906.

Subject. Walking with God.

Scripture Reading. Leviticus xxvi:3-13; II Corinthians vi-vii:1

<u>Text II Cor vi.16 "I will walk in them."</u>

Paul quotes from Scripture Leviticus 26, but the tabernacle there promised could not be the material one. The Lord is making a great promise: "My tabernacle (or residence) shall be among you."

But alas! That wonderful promise was conditional. It is "if ye keep my sabbaths etc." The promise is therefore dependent upon man. But when the fullness of the gentiles shall be gathered in then shall Israel be restored. God has raised up a church in place of a nation. The church is now the temple of God and God finds his home in her. Paul says "ye must be separated from the world."[273]

Most of us are more or less conversant with the thought of God dwelling in us. God reveals Himself and His goings in each individual saint. When God walks in me, I am walking in some measure worthily of God. It is not my simply making a desperate effort. Whatever God is, is to come out in my life. Oh what a humbling theme we have.

---

273 2 Corinthians 7:1.

I 1st John iv.16

Supposing that God walks about in me, what sort of life shall I lead? Of course if God is love, and God is going to walk in me, I must walk in love and love is to be the atmosphere that surround me on every side.

God walked in Jesus.

We may walk in truth without walking in love. You may walk in justice and you may walking integrity and yet all short.

II 1John 1:5

God is light and therefore if God walks in me my path must be a bright one. Luke 11 ver 36

Ah! Lord, this is where we break down and fail. A xian, is an illumination. He has to be transfigured like his Lord.

"Walk in light."

But light always means contrast.

Light always challenges attention.

Light is that which makes evil ashamed.

Depend upon it if God in whom is no darkness at all walks in you, His brilliancy will be coming out in your life.

Do you say "I wish with all my heart that I gave more light."

The burner and incandescent burner[274].

---

274 From 1885, gas lighting was improved following the development of the incandescent light by the Austrian, Carl Auer, Baron von Welsbach. His light worked on an entirely new principle. Whilst the light of flat flame and Argand burners was produced by raising the carbon particles in the gas to incandescence – that is, the flame produced the light - Welsbach used the atmospheric or Bunsen burner to create a hot blue flame. This gave no light itself but raised to incandescence the oxides of two rare metals: thorium and cerium in the proportion of 99% and 1% respectively. The incandescent gaslight was at least ten times more efficient than conventional burners, although the use of the lamps at

III John iv:24. Gal v16

Do you see how the thought holds good all the way through? The idea that we have of spirit is that of something which is not earthbound. "If ye walk in the Spirit ye shall not fulfil the lusts of the flesh."

IV Are there any other definitions of God? Psalm xlii:2

The peculiar character of Jehovah is life.

Romans vi:4 "walk in newness of life." i.e. a living walk.

Paul says that xians are the temple of God. But what sort of God?. Now if the living One walks about in me, what a wonderful life I shall lead, shall I not? The grand characteristic of the church of God must be life.

V Hosea xi:9

Can it be that this has any bearing upon the way in which I ought to walk. 1Cor iii:3

Then there ought to be something in our life that is altogether higher than that which belongs to man. It is for us to be able to say "Because I am not simply a man, but have God dwelling in me."

"I am God and not man." and hence where God walks in us there will be more than man in our lives.

---

first was hampered by the difficulty of replacing the extremely fragile mantles impregnated with the two rare metals. From about 1905 inverted incandescent burners became available: these had the advantage that the light shone downwards without creating a shadow.

Appendix II

FAREWELL ADDRESS:—

TO

MR. P. BRYANT.

Dear sir,

We, the teachers and students of American Baptist Mission Training School, as well as other friends of the same mission here, are exceedingly glad to give you an address on the eve of your departure from Bapatla to qualify yourself as a missionary in an American Training School. During your short stay here you won the appreciation of the Bapatla Public by your honesty and straight-forwardness. Your teaching of Sunday school lessons was very interesting, being full of faith and devotion.

Your preparation of students for athletic sports was admirable. A few days training under you made the students of this institution to win in the Tug of War with the High School boys who have had regular Gymnastic training under able and famous instructor. We, sincerely hope that you will come back to Bapatla as a missionary after undergoing a course in America and work among us.

May God be with you through your career and help you in your honest and noble attempts.

We remain,

Yours Sincerely,

[signatures]

K. Ramakrishnam church Head master

K. V. Ranga charlu Head master

M. V. Subharaou. 1st Asst

D. Venkateswara Sarma 2nd asst

N. Venkataswami Nayudu Sch. Board member Ongole

Jonnalagadda Samuel

M. M. a. David.

S. K. P. Press, Bapatla.

Farewell Address:-

To Mr P Bryant.

Dear Sir,

We, the teachers and students of American Baptist mission Training School, as well as other friends of the same mission here, are exceedingly glad to give you an address on the eve of your departure from Bapatla to qualify yourself as a missionary in an American Training School. During your short stay here you won the appreciation of the Bapatla Public by your honesty and straight-forwardness. Your teaching of Sunday school lessons was very interesting, being full of faith and devotion.

Your preparation of students for athletic sports was admirable. A few days training under you made the students of this institution to win in the Tug of War with the high School boys who have had regular Gymnastic training under able and famous instructor. We, sincerely hope that you will come back to Bapatla as a missionary after undergoing a course in America and work among us.

May God be with you through your career and help you in your honest and noble attempts.

We remain, yours Sincerely,

K Ramaknishman. Other names ....?

Appendix III

Names inscribed in Pencil in front cover of the diary

Mother

Miss H[275]

Fookes[276]

Mrs Welch

Mr Hutch

Mrs Yates

Mr W Dawbarn 28 Market Place Wisbech, Cam[277]

---

275 Is this Miss Hobson of Winchester, mentioned in the diary?

276 Maybe a Miss Fookes like Miss H? Fookes is a common Yorkshire name and is also found elsewhere in the UK.

277 The Dawbarns were a wealthy dissenting Baptist family in Wisbech. See W.F. Yeo, *William Dawbarn: A Victorian Life* (Canada: University of Victoria, 2011). William Dawbarn died 1881. William Y Jr (Grandson) 1872-1966 is possibly the only "W" eligible for the person mentioned here, but he lived in Liverpool. His son is Sir Simon Y Dawbarn, born 16 Sept 1923. There was a Dawbarn and sons Grocery and Drapery Shop in Wisbech Market Place in post WWI era.

Bibliography

Primary Sources

National Archives, Kew, Richmond, Surrey, TW9 4DU

> *WO 363 British Army WWI Service Records 1914-1920*
>
> *WO 364 British Army WWI Pension Records 1914-1920*
>
> *WO 372/3 Medical Card WWI 1914-1920*
>
> *1891 Census Returns of England and Wales*
>
> *1901 Census*
>
> *1911 Census*

York City Archives, York Explore, Library Square, York, YO1 7DS

> *York Municipal Register of Voters 1914-1915*

County Record Office, Malpas Road, Northallerton, North Yorkshire, DL7 8TB.

> *Thirsk and Malton Register of Voters 1918-1948*

Borthwick Institute for Archives, University of York, Heslington, York, YO10 5DD.

> *MRC.1/4/2 Quarterly Minutes of York Clifton Methodist Circuit (1888-1929)*
>
> *MRC.1/4/3 Quarterly Minutes of York Clifton Methodist Circuit (1930-1941)*
>
> *MRC.1/2/5 York Circuit Minutes of Committees*
>
> *MRC.1/2/6 York Circuit Minutes of local preachers meeting 1901-1925*
>
> *MR.HW.3 Wesley Guild Haxby minutes 1921-1962*
>
> *MR.Y/6/2 Minutes of Meetings of Committee of New Chapel (1883-)*
>
> *MR.Y/GRO.28 Groves Methodist Register of Marriages 1886-1922*
>
> *MR.Y/GRO.28 Groves Sunday School Minutes 1914-1927*
>
> *MR.Y/GRO.12 Groves Trustees Minutes 1883-1927*

Devon Heritage Services, Great Moor House, Sowton, Exeter EX2 7NL

DRO 2095D *Hatherleigh Methodist Circuit, circuit plans 1951-1959, Quarterly Circuit Meetings 1951 - 1959*

2399D/20 *Minute book of Quarterly Circuit Meetings, East Devon Mission.*

Voters Lists 1949-1963, Torrington District and Sidmouth.

Imperial War Museum, Lambeth Road, London SE1 6HZ.

41.22/3-8 A Soldier's Prayer

06/921 Private Papers Captain C. Tilston (Chaplain)

IP/MCR/75 Memoirs of R.F.E. Evans

The British Library, 96 Euston Road, London, NW1 2DB

Public Works Department Madras Presidency 1910-1911 Administration Report. Madras: Government Press.

Administration Report of the Public Works Department, Madras (General and Buildings and Roads) 1905-1906. Madras: Government Press.

Administration report of the Public Works Department (with a detailed review of Canal and Military Works) Madras Presidency 1906-1907. Madras: Government Press.

Regulations for the equipment of the regular army Part 2, Section XII, Garrison Artillery, Special Instructions and details. (1899). London: War office.

Royal Artillery Reading Room, The Royal Artillery Museum, Royal Arsenal, Woolwich, London, SE18 6ST.

Digest of Service, 52nd Coy RGA, previously 37th Coy (1906-1910).

H.A.G Digest 181st Heavy Artillery Battery, in the 96th Heavy Artillery Group, 100th Heavy Artillery Group, and 95th Heavy Artillery Group 1917-1919.

Secondary Sources

Anon. *Beaford: A Moment in Time.* (Beaford: Beaford Women's Institute, 2000).

n.a., *Forms of Prayer for public and private use in time of war* (London: SPCK,1915).

n.a., *Garrison Artillery Training Volumes I, II and III* (London: War Office, 1905-1910).

n.a., *Hymns for use at Services of Intercession during the war Sheet 11* (London: National Council of Evangelical Free Churches, n.d.).

n.a., *International Correspondence Schools Instruction papers reprinted* (Montana: Kessinger Publishing Company, 2003).

n.a., *Per Christum Vinces, Prayers in time of war* (London: Longmans, Green and Co., 1917).

n.a., *Regulations for the equipment of the Regular Army. Part 2 – Section XII, Garrison Artillery, Special Instructions and Details.* (London: War Office,1899).

n.a. "Sergeant Major", *The Cameliers* (London: Andrew Melrose Ltd., 1919).

n.a., *The Handbook of Artillery: including mobile, anti-aircraft and trench materiel* (Washington: Government Printing Office, 1920).

n.a. *The R.A.M.C. In Egypt.* (Toronto: Cassell And Company, 1918).

Anderson, David J., *Hartley to Seaton Sluice 1760 – 1960 The Military Connection* (Seaton Sluice: Seaton Design Group, 1990).

Armitage, Thomas, *A History of the Baptists* (New York: Bryan, Taylor and Co., 1890).

Balmer, Randall Herbert, *Encylopedia of Evangelicalism* (Louisville: Westminster John Knox Press, 2002).

Bebbington, David, *Evangelicalism in Modern Britain; A History from the 1730s to the 1980s* (London: Unwin Hyman, 1989).

Benstead, Charles R. Introduction by Cecil, Hugh, *Retreat, A Story of 1918* (Columbia: University of South Carolina, 2008).

Bhattacharya, Sabyasachi, *Education and the disprivileged, Nineteenth and Twentieth Century India* (Hyderabad: Orient Longman, 2002).

Brackney, H., *Historical Dictionary of the Baptists. Second Ed.* (Maryland: The Scarecrow Press, 2009).

Brown, Hilton (Ed.), *The Sahibs. The Life and ways of the British in India as recorded by themselves* (London: William Hodge and Company Ltd., 1948)

Carman, W.Y., *Richard Simkin's Uniforms of the British Army. Infantry, Royal Artillery, Royal Engineers and other corps* (Exeter: Webb and Bower, 1985).

Clarke, Dale, *British Artillery 1914-19, Heavy Artillery* (Oxford: Osprey Publishing, 2005).

Clough, John E., *From Darkness to Light: A Story of the Telugu Awakening* (Philadelphia. American Baptist Publication Society, 1892).

Caddell, Walter B., *Handbook for Proficiency Pay, Royal Garrison Artillery* (London: William Clowes and Sons, 1912).

Day, Henry C., *A Cavalry Chaplain* (London: Heath Cranton Ltd., 1922).

Day, Henry C., *An Army Chaplain's War Memories* (London: Burns and Oates, 1937).

Dennis, James S., *Christian Missions and Social Progress: A sociological Study of Foreign Missions, Vol III* (Toronto: Fleming, H. Revell Company, 1906).

Downes, R.M., *The Australian Army Medical Services in the war of 1914-1918 - Part II in Volume I (2nd Ed.)* (Canberra: Australian War Memorial, 1938).

Downie, David, *The Lone Star: The history of the Telugu Mission of the American Baptist Missionary Union* (Philadelphia: American Baptist Publication Society, 1892).

Downie, D., *The Nellore Station and field of the American Baptist Telugu Mission, South India 1922* (Philadelphia: American Baptist Publication Society, 1922).

Downey, Michael, *Understanding Christian Spirituality* (New Jersey: Paulist Press, 1997).

Duncan, F., *History of the Royal Regiment of Artillery Compiled from the original records Vol. 1 and II* (London: John Murray, 1879).

Farndale, Martin, *A History of the Royal Artillery: The Forgotten Fronts and the Home Base 1914-1918* (London: Royal Artillery Institution, 1988).

Fountain, David, *Lord Radstock and the Russian Awakening* (Southampton: Mayflower Christian Books, 1988).

Fox, H.E., *The Pope, the Kaiser and Great Britain.*(London: World Evangelical Alliance, 1914).

Frykenberg, Robert Eric, *Oxford history of the Christian Church, Christianity in India from Beginnings to the Present* (Oxford: Oxford University Press, 2008).

Gardiner, Juliet, *The Animals' War: Animals in Wartime from the First World War to the Present Day* (London: Portrait, 2006).

Gammell, William, *A History of American Baptist Missions in Asia, Africa, Europe and North America under the care of the American Baptist Missionary Union* (Boston: Gould Kendall and Lincoln, 1854).

Gregory, Adrian, *The Last Great War. British Society and the First World War* (Cambridge: Cambridge University Press, 2008).

Griffiths, P.J., *The British In India* (London: Robert Hale Ltd., 1946).

Hall, R., *Things are Different now* (Winchester: Winchester Famiily Church, 2008).

Hartley, Cathy, *A Historical Dictionary of British Women* (London: Europa Publications Ltd., 2003).

Headlam, John, *History of the Royal Artillery from the Indian Mutiny to the Great War 1899-1914 III volumes* (London: Naval and Military Press, 2005).

Hendrickson, Kenneth E. III, *Religion and the Public Image of the British Army, 1809-1885* (Cranbury, USA: Associated University Presses, 1998).

Henig, Ruth, *The Origins of the First World War* (London: Routlege, 2002).

Hildebrandt, Franz and Beckerlegge Oliver A. (Eds), *The Works of John Wesley Vol. 7* (Oxford: Clarendon Press, 1983).

Hogg, I.V., and Thurston, L.F., *British Artillery Weapons and Ammunition 1914-1918* (London: Ian Allen, 1972).

Holden Pike, G., *The Life and Work of Charles Haddon Spurgeon, Vol 5* (London: Cassell, 1894).

Holmes, Richard, *Sahib. The British Soldier in India 1750-1914* (London: Harper Collins, 2005).

James, Lawrence, *Raj. The Making of British India* (London: Abacus, 1998).

Keegan, John, *The First World War* (London: Hutchinson, 1998).

Keegan, John, *The First World War: An Illustrated History* (London: Hutchinson, 2001).

Kennedy, Dane, *The Magic Mountains: Hill Stations and the British Raj* (London: University of California Press, 1996).

Kincaid, Dennis, *British Social Life in India, 1608-1937* (London: Routledge & Kegan Paul, 1973).

Lapp, G.J., *The Christian Church in Rural India: A report on Christian Rural reconstruction and Welfare Service by the Christian Forces of India and Burma* (Calcutta: YMCA, 1938).

Massey, W.T., *How Jerusalem was won, being the record of Allenby's campaign in Palestine* (London: Edinburgh University Press, 1919).

Maurice-Jones, Col. K.W., *The History of Coast Artillery in the British Army* (London: Royal Artillery Institution, 1959).

McCasland, David, *Oswald Chambers: Abandoned to God* (Grand Rapids: Oswald Chambers Publications Association, 1992).

McPherson, Joseph D., *"Our People Die Well," Glorious Accounts of Early Methodists at Death's Door* (Bloomington, IN: AuthorHouse, 2008).

Montgomery, Helen Barrett, *Following the Sunrise: A Century of Baptist Missions 1813-1913* (American Baptist Publication Society, 1913).

Moule, H.C.G., *A Letter to British Soldiers: I Believe, I Belong* (Stirling: British Soldiers and Sailors Gospel Letter Mission, 1903).

Nason, Anne (Ed.), *For Love and Courage. The Letters of Lieutenant Colonel E.W. Herman from the Western Front 1914-1917* (London: Preface, 2009).

Page, Melvin E. (Ed.), *Africa and the First World War* (London: Macmillan, 1987).

Phinney, F.D., *The American Baptist Mission Press, Rangoon, Burma 1816-1908* (Rangoon: American Baptist Mission Press, 1909).

Phinney, F.D., *The Judson Centennial Celebrations in Burma 1813-1913* (Rangoon: American Baptist Mission Press, 1914).

Prescott, Nellie G., *The Baptist Family in Foreign Mission Fields. A Mission Study for Adults and young people* (USA: Judson Press, 1926).

Rinaldi, Richard A., *The order of Battle of the British Army 1914* ([ebook], Orbat.com, Tiger Lily Books for General Data LLC, 2008).

Robbins, Joseph C., *Following the Pioneers, A story of American Baptist Mission Work in India and Burma* (Philadelphia: Jusdon Press, 1922).

Salkeld H., *The Vital Year* (Harpenden: Gospel Standard Trust Publications, 1996).

Salmon, Thomas W., *The Care and Treatment of Mental Diseases and War Neuroses ("Shell Shock") in the British Army* (New York: War Work Committee of the National Committee for Mental Hygiene, 1917).

Sanday, W., *When should the war end?* (London: Evangelical Information Committee, 1917).

Secretary of State for India, *The India List and India Office List for 1902* (London: Harrison and Sons, 1902).

Sellers, William E., *With Our Fighting Men: THE STORY OF THEIR FAITH, COURAGE, ENDURANCE IN THE GREAT WAR* (London: Religious Tract Society, 1915).

Shedd, C. P., *History of the World's Alliance of Young Men's Christian Association* (London: SPCK, 1955).

Simpson, Capt. H.C.C.D., *The Garrison Gunner, (Regular, Militia and Volunteer)* (London: W.H.Allen and Co., 1890).

Skelley, Alan Ramsay, *Haxby in Wartime (1914-1918) and (1939-1945)* (York: Haxby Local History Group, 2004).

Smith, Tom (Ed.), *The Victorian Army at Home* (Montreal: McGill Queens University Press, 1977).

Smith, Tom (Ed.), *A History of Haxby, revised and expanded* (York: William Sessions Ltd., 2003).

Snape, Michael, *God and the British Soldier: Religion and the British Army in the First and Second World Wars* (London and New York: Routledge, 2005).

Spencer, William, *First World War Army Service Records. A guide for family historians, Fourth Edition* (London: National Archives, 2008).

Storrs, Ronald, *Lawrence of Arabia, Zionism and Palestine* (London: Penguin, 1940).

Varney, W.D., *A Short History of A.B.M Training School Bapatla, prepared for its Fiftieth Anniversary, Feb. 1939* (Philadelphia: American Baptist Publication Society, 1939).

Whitley, W.T., *The Baptists of London 1612-1928: Their Fellowship, their expansion, with notes on their 850 churches* (London: The Kingsgate Press, 1928).

Wiseman, Luke F., *Charles Wesley: Evangelist and Poet* (London: Epworth, 1932).

Witt, Fred Ralph, *Riding to war with "A". A History of Battery "A" of the 135th Field Artillery* (Virginia: Cleveland Evangelical Press, 1919).

Woodward, David, *Hell in the Holy Land: World War I in the Middle East* (Kentucky: American University Press, 2006).

Woodward, David, *Forgotten Soldiers of the First World War* (Stroud: Tempus, 2007).

Wort, R.S., *One hundred Years 1844-1914 The Story of the Y.M.C.A.* (London: YMCA, 1944).

Wright, John T., *An Evacuee's Story a North Yorkshire Family in Wartime* (Harbury Warwickshire: Lulu.com, 2007).

Journals and Periodicals

n.a., *91st Annual Report of the American Baptist Missionary Union, the Foreign Missionary Society of Northern Baptists 1904-1905* (Boston: American Baptist Missionary Union, 1905).

Carey, Benedict, On the Verge of "Vital Exhaustion"? *New York Times*, (31/05/2010).

Collen, Lieutenant General Sir Edwin, Section XI Army, *The Imperial Gazetteer of India, The Indian Empire, Vol IV* (Oxford: Clarenden Press, 1909).

Francis, W., *Gazetteer of South India, Vol 2* (New Delhi: Mittal Publications, 1988).

Hart, Lt. Gen. H.G., *Hart's Annual Army List militia list, and imperial yeomanry list for 1904* (London: John Murray, 1904).

Kelly's Directory of the North and East Riding of Yorkshire (London: Carey, Benedict, 1933).

Kinard, Jeff, *Artillery: An Illustrated History of Its Impact* (California: ABC-CLIO, 2007).

Pols, Hans and Oak, Stephanie, WAR & Military Mental Health: The US Psychiatric Response in the 20th Century. *American Journal of Public Health,* 2007 December; 97 (12): 2132–2142.

Walker, G.H.D., Section X Administrative, *The Imperial Gazetteer of India, The Indian Empire, Vol IV* (Oxford: Clarendon Press, 1909).

Yeo, W.F., *William Dawbarn: A Victorian Life* (Canada: University of Victoria, 2011)

ONLINE resources

n.a., Stations of British Troops in India, 19 November 1904, *Army and Navy Gazette:* http://usacac.army.mil/cac2/CGSC/carl/nafziger/904KAC.pdf

Animals in the Great War, www.firstworldwar.com/features/forgottenarmy.htm

Artillery Historical Books www.britishempire.co.uk/forces/armyunits/britishartillery/ra.htm

Bonser, Sapper H.P. *www.firstworldwar.com/diaries* Various diary records

Christian Herald 1902. www.oldandsold.com/articles24/speaking-oak-32.shtml

Dienstberger, Paul R. (2000) *The American republic a Nation of Christians,* (2000) www.prdienstberger.com/nation/Chap8wpr.htm

History Society of Southern Africa. uir.unisa.ac.za/bitstream/handle/10500/4627/Ragwan.pdf

Hogue, Oliver, *Turkish Prisoners in Egypt, A Report By The Delegates Of The International Committee Of The Red Cross* (1917) (Gutenberg, 2004, www.Gutenberg.org).

Mr Punch's History of the Great War: www.gutenberg.org/files/11571/11571-h/11571-h.htm

Purdom , C.P. (Ed) *From Everyman at War* (London: J.M.Dent, 1930). *www.firstworldwar.com/diaries/sapperinpalestine.htm*

Ragwan, Rodney (2011). *The narrative of the Baptist Association of South Africa and its significance for the Indian Baptist Church in KwaZulu-Natal.* Pretoria: Church

Smoking and 19th Century Evangelicals: www.spurgeon.org/misc/cigars.htm

Voices from WWI and connections to faith and the Bible www.biblesociety.org.uk/about-bible-society/our-work/world-war-1/

Online Images

Images of Palestine Campaign from New Zealand.
www.nzhistory.net.nz/media_gallery/tid/2225

Turkish photographs of the campaign.
www.turkeyswar.com/campaigns/palestine1.htm

A Brief history and Images, www.firstworldwar.com/battles/pf.htm

Images of the British in Jerusalem,
jerusalem-history.blogspot.com/2008/06/day-british-enterd-jerusalem.html

Library of Congress images of the Campaign.
memory.loc.gov/phpdata/pageturner.php?
Images=243&page=1&type=contact&agg=ppmsca&item=13709

The 60 Pounder Gun. www.hackneygunners.co.uk/the-gun-battery/the-gun/

The SS Caledonia, www.swanhellenic.com/library/ss-caledonia-13661.html

35924628R00109

Made in the USA
Charleston, SC
21 November 2014